B E N   D O R F M A N

E.A.M.P.

THE HIGHLY INTELLIGENT

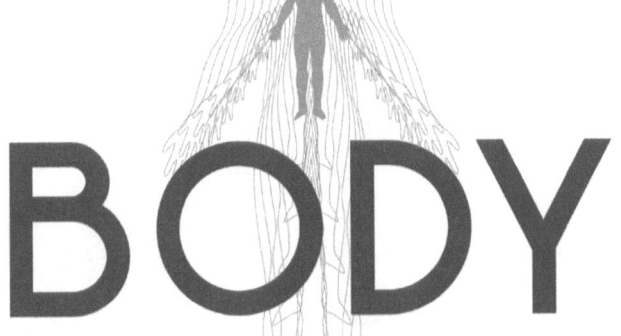

BODY

How Listening to Your Body Helps You
Heal and Connect to Your True Life Path

ABOUT THE AUTHOR

BEN DORFMAN is the owner and practitioner of **Seattle Acupuncture and Coaching, PLLC**, a clinic where he offers physical, emotional, and spiritual healing by combining acupuncture, life coaching, and energetic healing modalities. He has a deep passion for learning new healing modalities, especially ones linked to ancestral wisdom, and he is always in pursuit of deepening his relationship with spirit and Mother Earth. He lives in Seattle, Washington, with his wife and two children.

To schedule a healing session with Ben,
visit his website at
www.seattleacupunctureandcoaching.com

For updates about upcoming talks and seminars visit
www.thehighlyintelligentbody.com

CONTENTS

INTRODUCTION

Ever since I was a kid, I've never been able to understand all the suffering I've witnessed in the world. To this day, it breaks my heart that this suffering and unkindness have become such a normal way of living. I've always known in my heart that love and kindness towards one another are our natural ways of being.

When I was little, I asked my parents about the suffering around us, and although they had done their part to add kindness to the world, their response was simply, "This is just the way the world is." While we all have to come to terms with the suffering we witness, I have never been able to accept this as my normal.

As a result of the suffering I witnessed, and the personal suffering I experienced in my own life, I became deeply motivated to find the answers to heal my problems and spread more love into the world. It took me more than two decades of intense self-exploration to find all the pieces of the puzzle to help myself heal, and, to my surprise, it ultimately worked! Then I began to crave the ability to pass these tools along to others.

Fortunately, I chose a profession that allows me to help people who are going through issues similar to mine. The private practice I built is a blend of what I believe in my heart to be the most effective approach to treating emotional, physical, and spiritual problems all at once. I've been in practice now as an acupuncturist and life coach for more than a decade, and in that time, I've had the privilege of testing and honing the tools that work best for healing.

This book is my attempt to offer these tools to a broader audience in a way that's easily understood. They're given in a linear form, but in practice, they are all intuitive tools. There's no correct order for using them.

When people walk into my office, I always try to tune in to where they are in their healing journey and which tools are needed for them that day. I encourage you to listen to your own body as you read this book and notice what parts of it resonate with you. Trust your body, as it's your best guide for healing.

I've also decided to share my personal healing journey with you because I'm a big believer in the power of vulnerability. It can help us create deep connections with each other and help others heal. My story is imperfect because I'm an imperfect person, and I want us to view imperfection as normal, because in truth, no one is perfect.

I hope my story validates some of your own personal struggles and experiences, and I hope this book gives you some tools to guide you through your own healing.

My Story

From the first moment I was born into this world, I experienced pain. And not just the intense and discombobulating pain of physically being born, but another type of pain—like an atmospheric energy that was all around me.

This energy wasn't mine. I know this because I have a heart memory of myself as a spirit without a body. I can remember the sensations of how I felt—full of love, joyful, connected, and full of light. In comparison, this new, painful energy felt like heartbreak, sadness, heaviness, and disconnect. It was jarring and terrible to experience.

This was my initiation into the current human experience including my family's generational trauma, my parents' wounds, and their unmet needs. I know I'm not unique in my initiation. We all go through this at some point, but mine happened immediately and loudly.

All of this may sound dramatic because not many people remember themselves being born, let alone have memories of being a spirit. And honestly, I don't remember it visually. The memory is emotional in nature, a big feeling of truth that has always been with me.

Western culture doesn't always give credit to pure feelings because it wants some logical proof or reasoning, but as we will discuss later, feelings are highly accurate and are our best internal compass for finding the truth, including our true self.

What this original heart memory allowed me to see clearly was that something was wrong with my environment. I had no idea what the problem was or where the source of the pain lay, but I knew something wasn't right. I also felt disconnected from the loving source of light and energy that I knew to be home. This made me feel like I had been deliberately marooned on an alien island, alone without love. Could the loving source of energy—the oneness that I trusted above all else—deliberately disconnect itself from me and put me here to suffer? What a terrifying thought! "This can't be true!" I thought. "I know the loving source is real, and I know it loves me so deeply because I can still feel the memory of it in my heart." But as I looked all around me, I couldn't find it anywhere, so I felt heavy and alone.

Obviously, when we're so young, these feelings are impossible to communicate, let alone understand. So it took a long time for me to get the help and clarity I needed. I'm talking decades of searching.

In the beginning of our lives, it's our parents or primary caretakers we turn to for soothing, understanding, and guidance. They are our gods. I felt most connected to my mother because she was a healer (as I was meant to be) and because she suffered pain similar to what I suffered with regard to separation from the divine. Unfortunately, I could also feel from the very beginning that my presence in her life amplified her struggles and made it impossible for any of her needs to be met. Those were her own issues in her marriage and the active wounds she still carried, but I was impacted by this, which is what happens to all kids. My knowledge of this dynamic was communicated to me as a sadness and loneliness that was always in my body.

We're all born as sensitive radar systems that pick up the tiniest intricacies of the emotional dynamics around us. We express these findings outwardly for everyone to see so that, ideally, these emotional imbalances can be noticed and fixed. However, too often, the adults around us invalidate or misinterpret our expressions, especially in households where the parents still have their own emotional healing to do (which is in most households). Often this is not due to malicious intent, but because parents don't have the emotional awareness to understand what we are going through, or they are too consumed by their own pain, their own unmet emotional needs, and the need to survive in this world.

This was my experience as a child. I felt attuned to the unresolved wounds and pains of my parents. As a result, I strongly felt this emotional information in my body. This was communicated to me in various ways including through the tone of their voice, facial expressions, and the quality of their energy; or when my mom had terrible migraines. I had no idea how to communicate all of this to my parents, but I was overwhelmed and often in emotional pain.

During the day, I would be overly clingy, never wanting to be left alone. I'd often cry if I wasn't being held by one of my parents. And I'd cry all night long, every night for months on end. My poor parents!

Internally, I struggled with a constant feeling of grief and deep loneliness, as I felt misunderstood and unseen. For decades, I believed these feelings to be mine, but I would later find out that some of these experiences were feelings I had picked up from my environment—body indicators of what was happening around me. These feelings also represented the quality of closeness, or lack thereof, between my parents and myself at any given moment.

Our bodies speak to us via emotions, ailments, and thoughts. They constantly feed us information about the energy of the people, places, and things in our environment. If we listen to our body and try to understand what it's showing us, we see that it's a beautiful internal compass of all things—a highly supportive guide in this human world.

At the time, I wasn't aware of any of this and had no one to help me understand what was happening inside of me. To my parents' credit, they did all they could to help me. They discovered I was allergic to dairy products and took me off cow's milk, which greatly improved my sleep. It also prevented a lot of future ailments like asthma, eczema, and other respiratory and gastrointestinal (GI) challenges. When I was bullied in public school, my parents sent me to a private school, which put a lot of financial strain on them. Also, over the course of my childhood and adolescence, my mother took me to many alternative practitioners, including acupuncturists, chiropractors, therapists, shamans, and energy healers.

The Inner Bully

Unfortunately, despite their best efforts, things got worse as I got older. Towards the end of middle school, I started to have violent and hateful thoughts about myself. It was like the volume of my mind was turned up to 10, so I started to struggle with depression. It felt like I had another person inside my body—a bully who just wanted to harm me at all times. My thoughts screamed, "You suck! I fucking hate you! No one loves you!" or "You're a pathetic piece of shit. Look how weak you are!"

It escalated even further when I was introduced to toxic hypermasculinity in high school. The wounds and insecurities I carried were constantly triggered by this brand of masculinity, and it amplified my self-hatred. The thoughts in my head became comparisons to all the other men around me. I perceived them as bigger, cooler, stronger, and more masculine than I was. My mind would show me detailed images of girls I liked having sex with these men, not me. It was torture.

When we're faced with pain and trauma, we create amazing survival strategies. Our bodies are very intelligent in this way, making imperfect choices to function through dysfunction. On a physical level, I discovered I could function better and lift my spirits through female attention, sex, physical affection, and exhausting my body through intense physical activity. Of course, this meant that I had to cling to someone in a relationship at all times and could never be alone with myself. I deeply feared the moments I was alone, especially at night when I was supposed to be sleeping and resting.

On a mental level, I would create elaborate visual fantasies in my head that counteracted the brutality I was experiencing internally. These fantasies mostly involved being wanted by a woman or past girlfriend in some intense way, someone who was attracted to me. I fantasized about our sexual encounters, made up or real, all night long, and this provided a dopamine release for my body. It calmed me down, but it meant I was living in a fantasy world. As a result, I struggled more and more to exist as myself in reality.

All survival strategies are imperfect and have consequences. Usually, in the beginning we don't care about the consequences because we simply need to survive. But as time goes on, these mechanisms cause real problems, and we need help getting out of them.

By the time I started college, I was a mess. By my senior year, I had hit rock bottom. I was in so much emotional agony that I skipped classes and cried in my room all day until I found the strength to go to the gym. The self-hatred within me was so loud that I could no longer take it. I started having serious suicidal thoughts and was on the verge of killing myself.

My parents noticed and pulled me out of school. I returned home to finish my last semester at a college close to them. My mom fixed my diet and put me on supplements to ease my pain. (She's a wonderful nutritionist.) This definitely helped me feel better. I also started seeing my parents' therapist, hoping it would relieve my emotional pain. Unfortunately, it didn't. Over the course of four months, however, I was able to recover and go back to my normal baseline of just hating myself rather than wanting to kill myself. At the time, this felt like a huge improvement.

At that same time, I applied to and got into Bastyr University's acupuncture program in Seattle. I mentally prepared myself to live across the country in a place where I knew no one. Clearly, this was worrisome given what I was going through, but I tried to hold out hope that Seattle would give me access to new possibilities. I also got a wonderful puppy and named him Rockstar. He became my dearest companion and saved my life because I no longer had to be alone. Having him with me in Seattle was a tremendous help, and our daily walks in the woods became my new meditation.

I first arrived in Seattle about a month before class started, so I had a lot of empty time on my hands. Immediately, I started to search for different types of groups to join, knowing I needed consistent support in some way but not sure what kind of group would be best for me.

I eventually came across a group called "Practicing Living in the Moment." As I entered the meeting, I was met by a big, wonderful man whose energy and smile instantly put me at ease. It was a new and surprising feeling for me. Warren was the kindest and most vulnerable man I had ever come across, and he became a father figure for me. He opened up the circle that night by sharing about his past struggles with internal pain and alcoholism and how he was hoping to build a group of people who wanted to explore emotions, awareness, and healing together. What an incredible idea!

Up until that point, I didn't know that other people struggled with pain similar to my own, and I certainly didn't know there were tools to help. This became my weekly book group, where we read books out loud together and discussed our thoughts and feelings about them. The first book we read was *The Power of Now* by Eckhart Tolle, whose first chapter was entitled "You Are Not Your Mind." His ideas blew me away and created a mental and emotional awakening for me. I craved answers like never before. This would drive me to consume lots of information and try any experience that could offer me healing.

While I was having this passionate love affair with my mental, emotional, and spiritual sides, I was also going through a stressful and unsatisfying training program to become a Chinese herbalist and acupuncturist. I always loved the idea of energy medicine and had attended different energy medicine conferences in high school and college. I'd also tried many energy healers over the years, so I was initially excited to go to Bastyr and be thrown into a world of spirituality and energy healing.

In my mind, acupuncture was an ancient art form that was deeply linked to spirit and to something very deep within all of us. To my disappointment, the training was much more westernized and structured than I'd expected. There were no spirituality or intuitive teachings. About two years into the program, I started to have doubts about being there. I debated whether I should quit and become a therapist. I talked with my mother about it, and she encouraged me to finish my training and also become a life coach. This would allow me a platform to do emotional healing work with clients. The idea resonated with me, and I bit the bullet to finish the training.

After a couple of years of being in Seattle, I started to notice how much I was changing. The combination of walking through the woods each day with Rockstar and being part of the book group began to soften the hard exterior that I'd built over the course of my life. I started to allow myself to be more emotional, and I attracted people who made me happier. I slowly healed the toxic masculine ideas that I'd been taught. I began to express myself more by getting colorful tattoos and letting my hair grow long. Although these were all positive changes for me, I still struggled with depression, a fear of being alone, and a lot of negative self-talk. So far, with everything I was learning, nothing had changed that inner conversation. It wasn't until I met my wife, Sashya, that big shifts happened.

When I met Sashya, I knew I wanted to find someone mature, gentle, and kind who was working on themself. After a bunch of unsatisfying past relationships, I remembered that at my core, I'm a gentle person. This made me realize that in order to be myself I needed to be with a gentle person. With this new lens, I noticed completely new people, and when Sashya and I went on a blind date, I immediately recognized her as the type of person I wanted to be with. Fortunately, she felt the same way about me, so we started to build a life together.

Sashya is an amazing woman who is highly intelligent, emotionally deep, incredibly kind and someone who exudes love and playfulness wherever she goes. Her energy has this magical ability to pull you in, put you at ease, and make you feel seen. She is also quite outgoing by nature and seems to make friends with everyone she runs into. Being with her was natural and easy, and it was a great balance for my intense work ethic and my overall serious approach to life. I felt so lucky to be the guy she chose to give her love to.

From the start of our relationship, I knew I was going to struggle with my insecurities because this had always happened in romantic dynamics. I also knew instinctively that my insecurities might be even louder since I'd finally found a healthy person who loved me unconditionally. And this is exactly what happened. The negative and insecure thoughts in my head became so loud that they bombarded me every second of every day. Thoughts like "Sashya is so naïve, being all nice and loving towards me. Only children behave this way!" or "She's so full of shit, saying she loves me. She can't see how fucked up I am. She'd be so much happier with someone else." And images filled my head of her wanting partners from her past. If I wanted this relationship to last, I knew I needed help. That's when I came across two therapists who saved my life.

The first book I noticed when I was waiting in John's office was about attachment theory. It seemed interesting enough, and I had nothing to do. So I picked it up and started reading while waiting for a session. I had never heard of the ideas described in the book before, and I didn't know that John was an attachment-based therapist. I had chosen him because he was an older man with gentle, emotional energy, and I knew I had wounds with men.

As I read through the introduction of the book, it was as if someone had opened my mind and written about the painful shit in my head. I immediately knew that attachment theory was going to be an important part of my awareness and wound healing. Over the course of working with John for eight months, a part of me woke up. I started to understand how the quality of closeness that we experience as children, or lack thereof, creates our inner world and how we think about ourselves. It helped me begin to unravel some of my family's dynamics. This was the second time in my life that I felt the beginning of exponential emotional growth.

After about eight months, I still felt like I was missing something that John couldn't give me—some sort of direct mental awareness that would help me shift my relationship with my thoughts. I wondered how I could find another therapist who would know something deeper.

One day I had an idea. I knew I struggled with intimacy, both physical and emotional. Physical intimacy was so stressful for me. I was always in my head, worrying about my performance and deathly afraid that Sashya would leave me if I didn't constantly wow her with my masculinity and sexual abilities. And I was equally uncomfortable with emotional intimacy. Meanwhile, Sashya, who loved me very much, was so relaxed and loving towards me. In reality, I couldn't do anything wrong in her eyes. I wondered if there was a therapist who specialized in intimacy and who could help me heal on a deeper level.

That's when I discovered Jamie, an intimacy therapist. Her energy was so intense and direct that she cut right through the fog and bullshit in my head and made deep observations about me. I soon realized that not only did she have some emotional awareness that I needed, but her intensity and directness were what I had unconsciously wanted as well.

Jamie was masterful at pulling me out of my mind and connecting me to the root emotions that were tied to my thinking. I never saw my thoughts and feelings as one unit before—that my thinking was always a reflection of an emotional experience. This was an incredible realization because I was so consumed by my fantasy world and my painful, loud thoughts. I never considered that they were accurately reflecting something emotional. Now that I had someone who could hold that space and help me land in my body, I began to have my third emotional awakening.

Jamie helped me deepen my awareness about my family dynamics and wake me up to the baggage I'd taken on. She directly saw and validated all of my inner experiences that I'd always worried were just me being too sensitive or too intense. (I'd been told that a lot over the course of my life.) To have someone validate all of my inner experiences and connect them to something real felt like an act of God—a blast of love that I desperately needed.

The beauty of any thought or feeling is that you can work with it repetitively and have a multitude of discoveries and awakenings if you have the patience to not judge yourself. My projections of Sashya desiring other men were so all-consuming that I literally went into Jamie's office with the same projections every week for two years. She was so kind to me, never judgmental or exhausted by the repetition. Eventually, this hard work paid off, and my mind finally calmed down. I started to like myself for the first time in my life. This was unbelievable. I never imagined I could get there and feel so good! I had always assumed that those thoughts and painful emotions would eventually kill me. I estimated I wouldn't make it past age 26 or 27. But there I was at age 31— beginning to thrive!

Unfortunately, this feeling was short-lived due to the huge amount of change going on in my life. Sashya and I got married eight months after meeting, and by then, she was already pregnant. When I finished working with Jamie, I had two kids under the age of three. The problem was that Sashya and I couldn't find enough help with the kids, so we each ended up parenting our two babies while the other one worked. Every day we had to trade places, never seeing each other or having time to connect. I never realized how hard it was to have kids until I was in the thick of it, and I was totally overwhelmed, exhausted, and unhappy. I knew that my lifeline for happiness came from my close connection with Sashya, but even when we did see each other, we were too exhausted to enjoy it. I felt miserable and alone.

I didn't know how to communicate my unhappiness or what I really needed, so I shut down, worked a lot of hours, and tried to power through. Unfortunately, at that time, my successful acupuncture and coaching practice also began to have problems.

I had spent the better part of four years working my ass off to build my practice. By the time I met Sashya, I had a very full and successful business. This lasted until about three years into the relationship. Then, out of nowhere, everything slowed down. It was like someone turned off the valve that fed my practice energy and clients. At the same time, I decided to stop advertising on Yelp because it wasn't helping me find clients, and I watched as all my 5-star reviews disappeared. I had worked so hard to become the number one-rated acupuncturist in Seattle on Yelp, which was a big reason why I got so many clients. Having those reviews taken from me as a form of bullying and punishment only added to my misery. I spent most nights awake in a sweaty panic, worrying about becoming homeless or having to work for someone else, which was something I dreaded. Then, I'd wake up in the morning in a full-blown depressive state, wondering how my life had started to fall apart.

I was so stuck that I seriously thought of leaving my marriage and kids. I was overwhelmed with responsibility and had no idea how I could be happy as a family man. I had bought into the cultural romantic ideas of marriage, kids, and happiness.

People rarely talk about how hard it is, especially in a culture that makes you believe you have to do everything all on your own. I was so angry and cold to be around, giving Sashya and the kids no love. They didn't deserve that.

Then someone came into my life who injected hope and understanding back into my body. I'd always had big dreams of writing books and giving talks on emotional healing and awareness to large groups of people. This woman saw that potential in me and offered to help me accomplish it. No one had ever believed in me in this way. It gave me a massive jolt of energy for life, which I desperately needed. I was feeling so down about my business and thought maybe it was the universe's way of telling me that I needed to do something bigger. I felt very drawn to create something great with her and was on the verge of running away to a new life.

This person also helped me solve the issues in my business. I moved my entire practice to the south end of Seattle, close to where I lived. I got new business photos for my website, started an Instagram page, and was well on my way to finding a new version of myself. Moving was a huge help, and the flood gates of clients opened again after a year and a half of struggling. I was officially back in alignment with my life.

But something didn't feel right. Every time I thought about leaving Sashya and the kids, a huge feeling of loneliness washed over me. I worried that being away from them would be the biggest regret of my life. That's when a client of mine told me about ayahuasca.

Ayahuasca is a powerful plant medicine that has been used in the Amazon by indigenous tribes for thousands of years. It's a conscious plant spirit that helps you purge bad energy, heal addictions, and heal deep wounds through hallucinations and vomiting with the help of traditional plant medicine songs. It's taken with a group of people, all of whom need help of some kind, and with a traditionally trained shaman who sings the songs. If used with the appropriately trained practitioners, it has the potential to bring about profound healing. I was so blessed to have a client tell me about it.

I decided to give it a shot, because at that point, I had nothing to lose. I went into it with the intention of getting clarity about my marriage and my life as a whole. I was scared shitless, worried that the ayahuasca would make me lose my mind and myself.

As I drank it, I visibly shook, consumed with panic and anxiety. But after the medicine became active in my body, I saw a beautiful rainbow fabric like a spider web connecting everyone in the room. As I breathed out, the fabric vibrated, and I could sense how energetically entwined we all are as humans. This immediately put me at ease. Then I heard a voice say, "Don't worry. You can trust me."

From that point forward, I was totally open to the experience. The clarity I ultimately received was that my wife and kids are my wellspring of love in my life, and I'm at my best when I'm with them. It helped me reconnect on a body level to the love I felt for them, as well as to the love that was all around me. I also purged a bunch of cloudy, darker energies from my body during the ceremony, which resulted in the feeling that I was waking up from a bad dream. I felt happy and content for the first time in a very long while, and I desperately wanted to reconnect to my family. I was also told that I needed to end my connection with this other person as it was getting in the way of what really mattered—my relationship with my incredible wife and kids. I came home from the experience clearheaded, healed, and ready to work on fixing my marriage.

My wife and I spent the next two years doing a lot of grieving and healing work. This shifted much in our relationship, as we became extremely honest with each other about how we felt and what we wanted. Additionally, after the ayahuasca ceremony, I no longer experienced any depression. I was happier, lighter, more loving, and more playful with everyone. This was a big surprise for me and quite jarring for Sashya, who was now married to a completely different person. But these were all part of a big and wonderful change that was happening in our lives.

At the same time, my practice exploded with new clients, and I was busier than I'd ever been in my entire life. It was the first time that I truly felt satisfied and aligned with myself.

The following year, I went back to do my second round of ayahuasca at a three-day retreat, where we would drink and have a ceremony each night. I was nervous about it, given the fact that I'd just gone through a hard transformation. But I knew that ayahuasca could help me heal deep wounds I was still carrying. I decided to return with the intention of healing my grief with my mother and family, hoping to mend my broken heart. This was a big undertaking, because that grief was so entrenched in my body that I wasn't sure how much could be cleared in one weekend.

To my disappointment, on the first and second night I experienced very little healing and few visual images. Part of the reason you're required to do a three-night retreat is because it can take that long to build a good relationship with the plant medicine and for the ayahuasca to prepare your body for healing. Before the third ceremony, I was offered a chance to drink an extra dose an hour before the ceremony started, which could amplify the experience. And holy shit! Did I have an experience!

When the ayahuasca started to break through my grief, I was called to sit in front of the two shamans at the ceremony and have a medicinal song sung directly to me. I was feeling quite stuck, and I hoped the shamans could help me break through.

The song started to work its magic, and I began to cry out loudly, emotionally purging the grief from my body. This was followed by physical purging. Afterwards, I felt exhausted and relieved that I had been able to accomplish what I'd gone there for.

As it so happened, a mother and son were also attending the retreat together. This is the magic of ayahuasca. It seems to bring together the right people to accomplish healing for everyone in the group. As I went back to my mat, feeling accomplished, the mother and son were called up to sit in front of the shamans together. I heard a voice in my body say, "This is for you." I could feel in the moment how the plant spirit had made this happen for me, and I was shocked to have such a powerful setup for healing. As the shamans sang to the mother and son, I could feel something large wanting to be purged from my body. It was intense, and the ayahuasca kept telling me to look the other way as it took control of my body to help me heal.

I felt so sick that I had to get onto my hands and knees as I tried to vomit this thing out of me. I felt like a snake who detaches its jaw to eat its prey, and as I opened my mouth wide, I purged what I saw in my mind's eye as a large, calcified egg into my bucket. While there was no real egg, in my altered state I heard it land with a thud in the bucket. No wonder it took me three days and an extra dose to accomplish this!

The ayahuasca also helped me experience the love and spirituality of the Earth. I was wrapped up by Mother Earth as she filled my spirit with love. I had never felt unconditional love and safety like that before, and for the first time in my life, I was truly in a state of peace. There was much more to be shown and to learn that night before I was finished, more than eight hours later.

After that, so much started to change in my life. The biggest thing was that I found a healer and mentor who guided me to a teacher from the Lakota tradition (and many other traditional lineages). This person could train me to become a medicine man, a shaman, and a spiritual healer. It felt like everything I had ever wanted, allowing me to stay in deep connection with spirit every day. As I write this, I'm still in my first year of this training.

I wanted to tell my story before diving into the teaching part of the book, because I believe our personal stories are a powerful way to bring connection and closeness between people. Our stories can convey information, validate our experiences, build intimacy, and create healing.

I also wanted to set an intimate and honest tone in the book, being transparent about my struggles, imperfections, and mistakes. Yet through my imperfections, I've been blessed to find many emotional tools, which I've brought into my acupuncture and coaching practice for over 10 years and which I've used to help my clients. I can confidently say that the emotional tools I present in this book can help you heal on a physical, emotional, mental, and spiritual level, just as they've done for me and my clients.

When I say "help," I don't mean that you have to go through 10 years of therapy to find relief. These tools are designed to have immediate impact. I should also add that I don't claim to be the originator of any of these ideas, as they have all been around for millennia. But these are the ideas that helped me the most when I was suffering, and I hope some of them may bring you the same relief.

May the biggest and brightest version of yourself be brought into this world!

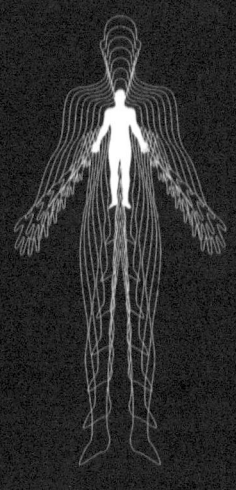

SECTION 1

AWARENESS-BUILDING

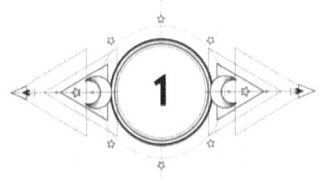

WE ARE ALL SENSITIVE CREATURES
WHO NEED LOVE TO THRIVE

The first step of awareness on our emotional healing journey is understanding how badly we need love and what happens to us when we don't have it. Culturally, when we talk about basic needs, we tend to mention physical things like food, shelter, water, clothing, education, healthcare, and a basic living income. These are all very important, but why haven't we elevated our core emotional needs to the same level of importance? We need to take them more seriously, because they're vital to our overall happiness and wellbeing. No wonder so many Americans struggle with insecurity, depression, anxiety, and loneliness!

We have an incredibly important and loud need to be loved, wanted, and cared for. We also need to feel important to the closest people in our lives. And we need to have caretakers who offer close, intimate connections full of warmth, tenderness, and emotional awareness.

Some of you may be thinking, "This level of love doesn't exist in this world." It's true that our world has become terribly deficient in love and tenderness. It's why people commit so many destructive acts on a daily basis to others, to animals, and to this wonderful Earth. But that's all the more reason why we must take our core emotional needs seriously and contribute to bringing love back into our lives and the lives of others.

We're all born into this world as tender, emotional, and loving creatures in deep need of bonding with a caretaker, not just to have our physical needs met, but also our emotional ones. Many studies over the past 75 years have proven this, although the earlier ones from the 1950s were conducted with animals in cruel ways. One example is the famous rhesus monkey experiments done by Harry Harlow in the 1950s, which proved that the monkeys preferred warmth and connection over just food and physical sustenance.

The quality of attachment (or connection) that you were given as a child greatly influences everything in your life including how you perceive and treat yourself, the internal dialogue you hear in your head, and your ability to connect with life and with others. This is because we each develop our sense of self and the world based on what we experience in childhood, whether healthy or unhealthy. We think our upbringing is "normal" until we're exposed to alternative dynamics that create opportunities for us to evaluate whether our "normal" is actually healthy or not.

American culture deeply values independence, so it tends to downplay our intense *dependence* on others, or how we create our sense of self based on the important people in our lives. What this means is that we naturally adapt our sense of identity in order to fit in, happily changing who we are to accomplish the bonding with others we desperately need.

Once we've found a version of ourselves that works, we tend to hold onto this identity long-term. For example, take someone who grew up in an environment that was highly competitive, in which high achievements were valued the most. If they were able to keep up with that high standard (and not everyone can), their approach to life would center around accomplishments and a strong desire to always win. However, if we track the origins of this identity, the person wasn't born that way. This competitiveness was built in them until it became their operating system.

The challenge is that these unconscious adaptations are incredibly hard to spot unless they cause us pain or suffering in some way. In the example above, if this person was unable to feel like a "winner," they might suffer from depression and self-hatred. Only through awareness-building would they be able to evaluate whether their early adaptations, and the family system they come from, were healthy for them or not.

But even as we heal and find healthier ways of operating, we still end up creating new versions of ourselves based on the influences of others. Our dependence on other human beings is very natural for us. We're simply a connection-oriented species, and we will always mirror our sense of self based on the people around us. This natural inclination isn't actually the problem. After all, it's been shown scientifically that groups of people who are part of strong and close communities tend to live longer, to be healthier, and to experience a happier life.

The issue is *who* we allow to be our mirrors and influencers. Ideally, we want to surround ourselves with emotionally healthy people. With this in mind, think of the terrifying role social media influencers currently play in our culture. The fact that there's such a role as an "influencer" shows how our thinking can be influenced by someone we idealize. Obviously, our innate craving for connection must be taken seriously, because it's one of the biggest influences that determines who we are.

When we're young, we don't have control over our caretakers, so we're at the mercy of our environment. Depending on our situation, this can be quite painful or emotionally damaging. But as we grow older and gain autonomy, we get to choose the types of relationships that feel best for us. Still, choosing healthier connections isn't so easy, because too often we get stuck in emotional patterns that are similar to the ones in which we were raised. It's only when we learn about healthy standards and listen to how our body guides us that we can make better choices and feel happier.

Attachment Theory

Understanding attachment theory is the first step in emotional healing. It can help us understand the quality of connections that we experienced as children and how they influenced the way we think of ourselves, as well as how we feel in relationships with others and the world. Depending on the types of attachments we experience, we have to adapt who we naturally are in order to maintain our connections with our parents, caretakers, and others who are important to us. We also mirror how our parents behave in their relationships and lives. Further, we tend to normalize how we're treated by them and use all of these factors as templates in our subsequent relationships.

All of this makes attachment theory a powerful resource for answers to our trauma and emotional struggles. We first need to dive into the dynamics of attachment so that we can better understand ourselves.

There are four attachment styles, and most of us have a mixture of them: secure, anxious (anxious-ambivalent), avoidant (anxious-avoidant), and disorganized (fearful-avoidant).

1. **SECURE ATTACHMENT** is the ideal and healthy version of how we show up in a relationship. When we're young, this occurs when we have one or more caretakers who are open, warm, emotionally aware (or in the process of growth and healing), and loving in the ways we need. They truly want to

be close to us, and we're important to them. With this type of person, we can feel safe expressing our feelings and being authentic. They also provide the help we need to understand and process our feelings. All of this helps to regulate our nervous system, a key function of being in a secure relationship. From this dynamic, we learn that our authentic self is good and valuable, and we become confident about who we are and how we feel.

People who come from secure environments also feel comfortable with intimacy, close connection, and showing up in the world as themselves. They have high resiliency and naturally gravitate towards healthy relationships. They tend to have an easier time loving themselves, and their inner dialogue is kinder to them. We can feel when we're in the presence of someone who's secure in themself because they tend to elevate the people around them. We naturally feel grounded in their presence.

2. **ANXIOUS ATTACHMENT** stems from a parent/child relationship in which love and connection are inconsistent. This means that the parent is attuned to the child's needs only part of the time, while other times the needs go unmet. This is confusing for children because it sends mixed signals about their parents' ability to show up for them. On the one hand, it seems like the parent is capable and available for connection. On the other hand, the parent seems incapable of understanding what the child needs in order to feel loved and secure. Oftentimes this creates a consistent feeling of anxiety since the child never knows if their needs will be met or if their main source of connection will be available to them.

Every time the parent withdraws emotionally, the child feels it as a loss. These little painful moments build up over the course of youth and adolescence and can sometimes cause covert emotional trauma (we'll discuss this topic in greater detail later in the book). As the parent or caretaker is sometimes emotionally distant, the child tends to become clingy out of the fear of losing the connection. For young children, who desperately need love and connection to survive and thrive, this relationship can be quite painful, both physically and emotionally.

At the root of this dynamic, a child never knows if they will feel loved by the closest person to them. When connection isn't available, kids will naturally blame themselves, thinking they did something wrong to cause the parent to withdraw. Surely, they think, if they were lovable enough (or more perfect in some way), their parent would never withdraw love. This dynamic promotes a self-hating and highly critical inner dialogue due to the inaccurate conclusion kids draw about the situation—that something is inherently wrong with them. It can also create a perfectionist mentality.

Furthermore, the anxious dynamic we experienced in our family system sets the stage for how we feel in future relationships. Anxiously attached people tend to become clingy, high-maintenance adults who need constant reassurance that their partner (or close people) still loves them. This is because they have deep insecurities about their own self-worth, which cause them to constantly fear being left by the people they love.

Additionally, anxious attachment can be caused by a reversal of roles with a caretaker, where the child feels they have to take care of their parent's emotional needs in order to get their own needs met. This happens when the parent's emotional needs have gone unmet, so they're in desperate need of connection themself. They use the relationship with their child (or children) to meet their own needs.

Another version of this might be a parent who is overbearing and too involved in their child's life, relying on this intrusive version of closeness to satiate their own need for love, validation, and connection. This whole setup is a reversal of roles because in a secure relationship, the emotional needs of the child get priority, and the caretaker looks to other adults for their needs to be met. A child doesn't have the capacity or knowledge to meet an adult's emotional needs, especially when they are young, so being asked to do so will only create unhealthy beliefs and emotional patterns in the child.

The child's need for closeness and connection can be a trigger for this type of parent, making them feel the child is too demanding. This reaction stems from the pain and longing the parent feels from never having their own emotional needs met. The thought of having to meet someone else's needs when they so badly crave this for themselves can result in a feeling of resentment, depression or irritation towards the child. Furthermore, watching a child's needs get met can also trigger jealousy.

If a child gets mad at their parent, this can be also trigger the adult, depending on how much they rely on the love and closeness of their child. For example, in a moment of frustration, a child might say "I hate you" to their parent. If this parent is already struggling to feel good about themself, this can be more deeply hurtful than it would be for a healthy adult. If this happens, kids may learn quickly to hold certain feelings back in order to keep the peace and preserve closeness with their parent. Over time, this trains the child to feel uncomfortable with fully expressing and being themselves.

When a child monitors the emotional needs of their parents and sacrifices their own needs and expression, it's often due to a narcissistic family dynamic. In this case, the parent is too consumed with their own unmet needs to fully show up for the child. This can give the impression to the child that their needs are less important than the needs of others or that they are inherently less important as a person. They might also think something's wrong with their authentic feelings.

Narcissism tends to be viewed in a negative light in our culture due to the overt versions we witness on social media, in politics, and in unhealthy interactions with each other. But we all have narcissistic parts of ourselves, which are just unmet needs and wounds. Too often, we don't talk about these subtler forms of narcissism.

When our emotional needs are unmet in childhood, it is often due to unconscious behavior on the part of parents who are good and kind people. Their intention is certainly not to harm us. However, regardless of intention, these interactions can still be harmful and cause emotional wounds over time. For example, someone who comes from a narcissistic family dynamic may struggle with depression, anxiety, or lack of self-worth despite what they felt was a wonderful upbringing. To them, their emotional pain doesn't add up. Yet, if we track the emotional dynamics of their family system, we will usually see that their emotional needs weren't met for a long time. Symptoms in the body point us to the truth of what happened. Usually, if we can't figure out why our pain is there, it's due to covert emotional trauma. In more extreme situations in can also be due to overt trauma that our body won't let us remember.

Of course, this doesn't mean that parents have to be perfect to avoid wounding their kids. It's not likely that an individual moment will cause trauma unless it's overtly violent or overtly harmful. Long-term, subtle harm can cause wounding, particularly when it accumulates over time without any attempt at repair.

3. The **AVOIDANT** or **ANXIOUS-AVOIDANT** attachment style involves a parent who has difficulty with emotional expression and closeness. Whenever their child needs emotional connection, the parent becomes uncomfortable and distances themself. In this kind of household, there is little tolerance for the expression of emotions, including joy and excitement. Furthermore, there is no place to be received and experience warmth. Children learn quickly, and painfully, that they have to hide their feelings and take care of their emotional needs for themselves. These children become adults who are incredibly independent and who struggle with intimacy. They're afraid to ever rely on others for help or connection. They suppress their feelings, which they equate with weakness. Due to this dynamic, they assume that no one is reliable or can be trusted.

Avoidant people may inaccurately appear to be secure, while in reality, they lack the skills to create connections with others, even if they desperately want them. Avoidant kids can be loners who deliberately choose to isolate themselves because it feels normal to them. They also do it to protect themselves from hurt. If you've ever seen a child who always plays alone, away from the group, this is likely a kid from an avoidant household. Learning to live without love is enormously painful, and self-isolation is difficult to maintain, because it goes against every natural instinct and craving in our body, mind, and spirit.

There is a film that drives home the pain that a child has to go through to become avoidant—the pain of having no love. It's called *A Two-Year-Old Goes to Hospital* by Robertson Films. It's a heart-wrenching documentary about a girl who went to the hospital for a minor operation and had to stay for eight days at a time when parents weren't allowed to go in with kids. Sometimes, visitations were allowed for just one hour each week. This young child didn't understand why her parents had abandoned her, and she had no familiar person to cling to. The movie shows her going through the deep grief and pain of the perceived loss of her caretakers and everything she knows. Imagine the panic! Over the course of her time at the hospital, the audience can visibly see the changes this girl undergoes compared to how she seemed when she first arrived. When her mother returns, she no longer trusts her mom the way she did before. The viewer witnesses how emotionally closed off and distant the girl becomes. This short documentary, paired with Rene Spitz's movie, *Grief, a Peril in Infancy*, had a big impact on the medical community in the 1950s, when attachment theory was still being developed.

Nothing will rip your heart apart faster than seeing the loss of love on a child's face. It becomes obvious how badly all of us need it. When we become adults, we tend to forget that we were once those vulnerable little children and that the effects of our childhood are still with us.

On a body level, being avoidant of love and connection always brings physical and emotional consequences. This is because our body is designed to help us get the love we need. It takes considerable effort to resist our natural craving for love and connection. This resistance causes us to constantly fight against our body's natural energy flow. Common symptoms of this battle are chronic tension, chronic pain, and fatigue. Closing love off from our body always translates into pain and emotional and mental turmoil. This can lead to further physical symptoms like chronic headaches, migraines, pre-menstrual cramping, fibromyalgia, digestive pain/issues, chronic fatigue syndrome, hypertension and/or rheumatoid arthritis. Resulting emotional turmoil may include chronic anxiety, insomnia, depression, addiction, and/or a mind that's always active. These are just some examples of how our body speaks to us when we're misaligned with what's healthy.

4. The last type of attachment is **DISORGANIZED ATTACH-MENT** or **FEARFUL-AVOIDANT**, which involves a child who lives in fear of their caretaker, someone who is highly inconsistent and unpredictable. This may be an adult who physically, emotionally, or sexually abuses the child or others around the child. Trauma comes from both experiencing such abuse and/or witnessing it. The child is emotionally torn, wanting and needing closeness with their caretaker while also rejecting any close proximity to the adult out of fear.

Disorganized attachment manifests in an adult as someone who's afraid of intimacy and who avoids closeness. This is similar to what occurs with avoidant people; however, they still crave relationships. Their trauma is projected onto their partners, and as a result, they expect rejection and pain. If they aren't conscious of these projections, they may behave in ways that harm their relationships. They might choose partners who recreate their wounding pattern and cause them to feel afraid. These people are at high risk for mental illness and aggressive behavior. They may even abuse their own children in the same ways that they experienced. This kind of wound is a challenge to heal, but it can certainly be done. It simply requires a lot of emotional support.[1]

The quality of attachment we experienced as kids sets the foundation for how we feel about ourselves, how we show up

---

1 The Attachment Project, "Attachment Styles & Their Role in Relationships," Accessed September 5, 2022, https://www.attachmentproject.com/blog/four-attachment-styles/.

in relationships, and how we relate to the world. Learning about our family's emotional dynamics and discovering how much of our emotional needs were met can shine a light on the emotional patterns we experience in adulthood. As we develop this awareness, we can also prevent the spread of these patterns to our children.

As you might have noticed in the descriptions above, most people's attachment style comes from parents with the same kind of attachment wounding. Healing this for ourselves not only deepens our emotional awareness, but it also promotes generational healing.

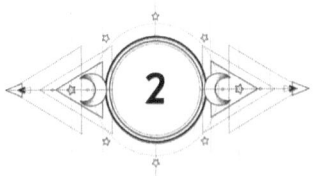

THE BODY IS OUR GUIDE

eing born with a body is a sacred gift. Not every spirit gets to have a body, so for those of us who do, it's something to be cherished. This may sound strange if you've never given it much thought, but we are spirits—beings of light. Each of us is a conscious piece of the same great, unconditionally loving creator; a universal energy I call Divine Mother. We come down here to inhabit this Earth in order to have opportunities to experience wonderful new things, to grow spiritually, and to help this planet and the human species to heal and evolve. We're able to do all of this only because Divine Mother and Mother Earth work together to provide us with these incredible vehicles called bodies, which allow us to experience life.

Giving your body the spiritual credit it deserves opens up a lot of opportunities to deepen your knowledge about how it operates as a highly intelligent and sensitive piece of earthly equipment. You can trust it deeply to guide you through life and healing.

Most of us aren't taught how our body operates on a physical, emotional, mental, and spiritual level. Instead, we tend to be thrown into life without knowing how to properly use this incredibly helpful system. Without this knowledge, life can feel very overwhelming. It can also be traumatic and harmful until we get used to it. Ideally, our culture should provide us with traditions, life wisdom, initiations, and ceremonies to help us understand how our body works and how to develop a wonderful relationship with it. But that isn't the case for most of us in the western world.

This chapter provides the knowledge you need to understand your body at a deeper level.

The Body Is Highly Sensitive and Energetically Attuned

Your body is highly sensitive to the emotional and energetic dynamics that are always around you. What this means is that it picks up on how other people feel internally about themselves, about you, and about the world. It also notices the wounds, traumas, and unmet needs of others. People's thoughts and feelings are always expressed outwardly in both obvious and subtle ways, and our body tracks all of it in the present moment.

There are endless ways that people express how they feel: via what they say, how they dress, how they move, and how they react in the moment, just to name a few. From a subtler perspective, people also express themselves through their facial cues, smell, tone of voice, movement of their eyes, and the aura that surrounds them. This is just the tip of the iceberg, but as you listen and tune into these things, the amount of information you begin to notice is incredible. And the body is conscious of all of it.

Our body also picks up on past energies in any environment, which includes the way people have felt or the experiences/events that unfolded in the past. Then, our body communicates this information to us in a variety of ways.

When we're young, the main people and environments we experience are our family and home. Our family system carries a lot of information like familial emotional patterning, generational traumas and wounds, familial beliefs about the world, and ideas about who we should be. All of this is expressed through our interactions and relationships with our parents or main caretakers, as well as through the family members around us in our younger years. The physical environment where we grow up also contains a lot of information about our family and community. In this way, our family dynamics are unconsciously and consciously passed down to us throughout our childhood. Our body is highly aware of this and knows which interactions and beliefs are healthy or unhealthy for us.

To give a few real-time examples of how our body tracks information, think back to a time when you walked into someone's house and felt instantly uncomfortable. Was there anything obvious that would explain the feeling? How about the opposite when you felt immediately at ease and safe in a new environment? The same can be said about people we meet. We either feel drawn to them, neutral about them, or uncomfortable around them. How does our body know to feel this way, even with people and places we know nothing about? This illustrates the intense energetic awareness of the body. It picks up on the energy around us immediately.

Another example is an experience where your external and internal worlds don't match. For instance, did you come from a family that seemed picture-perfect on the surface, full of love and closeness, yet you felt alone, anxious, or depressed? What about amongst friends? Have you ever been with your friends while they're having a great time, yet you feel alone, unhappy, depressed, or anxious? This can be your body talking to you about the group dynamics and the degree to which your emotional needs are being met, or not met, within that group.

Our bodies do this all the time, but we haven't been trained to listen to the information or trust its accuracy. The next time you're out and about, see what thoughts and feelings arise within you as you interact with different people and environments. What information is your body giving you in these moments? Through listening and giving credit to your feelings you can begin to repair your relationship with your body and start building a good foundation for your life.

The Body Operates on an Emotional Level

The body also functions on an emotional level in the way it absorbs and integrates information and the way it talks to us. This is because, as a species, we human beings are highly emotional, feeling-based creatures. Yet, the fact that we put so much value on logic over how we feel only goes to show how disconnected we are from ourselves.

When we were little, we learned a vast amount of information about the world based on how we felt. We could feel in our bodies whether there was love or warmth in our household and whether our parents were available for close connection. We also instinctively knew what we needed to do in order to become closer to our parents, as well as what behaviors would drive them further from us. We learned which emotions were "good" or allowed and which ones weren't, depending on how we were made to feel after expressing those emotions.

We could also feel who our parents wanted us to become and what they wanted us to believe. All of this happened on an emotional level—a highly intuitive place within us.

In this way, our body teaches us what we need and what's important by guiding us via our feelings. For example, as I've mentioned, if our emotional need to feel loved isn't fulfilled, our body manifests symptoms such as depression, loneliness, anxiety, or feeling unlovable. A second example is someone who is highly sensitive and emotional but was brought up in a household in which emotions were deemed "weak." This person's body might communicate to them that something isn't right by giving them chronic headaches or body tension, built-up anger, depression, or a desire to never be home.

Here's an opposite example. Let's say you feel an incredible surge of energy, happiness, and excitement every time you play music with your friends. This is your body giving you signs that you're aligned with what you need to feel nourished and loved.

Knowing that our body operates on an emotional level also gives us access to healing our emotional wounds in more efficient ways. Logic, and trying to have control over our mentality, will never work as a long-term strategy for healing because the body craves something deeper. The question we should be asking when it comes to shifting someone's feelings is "What emotional experience do they need to have in order to feel different?"

For example, if someone has a deep feeling of loneliness that seems to haunt them wherever they go, even if they have a ton of friends or a good family, what they need to feel different is to be seen and understood in a way that matters to them. Any other attempts at supporting them by using logical arguments, such as "you have so many people who love you," won't be effective.

Our bodies talk to us constantly via how we feel, and we need to practice listening to the messages and operating more on this level.

Our Thoughts Are Reflections of Our Feelings

Our thoughts and internal dialogue are reflections of our emotional experiences. What this means is that our thinking is deeply linked to our core emotional needs, whether those needs have been met, and how we've adapted throughout our life. Our thoughts are our roadmap through time, telling our story and revealing our emotional wounds.

Our body uses thinking to distance us from the emotions

that are too painful for us to fully experience until we have the resources and support to process them. Further, we use the power of our mind to control and influence the feelings that cause us grief, discomfort or harm. In this regard, our thinking is part of a survival system that helps us live with ourselves and get through the toughest parts of our lives.

Clearly, there are many helpful functions of our logical mind that we use on a daily basis, but the painful dialogue in our heads always reflects our emotional experiences.

Too often, we attempt to change our thinking without acknowledging the origins of the thoughts and the messages that our body is sending us on an emotional level. Instead, we can sometimes judge these thoughts as silly, stupid, or random. For example, in my practice, I've heard countless people say that their life is great and there's no reason for them to have unhappy thoughts in their heads. But our body is highly intelligent and never random, and it will never give us thoughts for no reason.

Many healing strategies attempt to shift our thinking by forcing new thoughts into our heads or by resisting thoughts that we don't want to listen to. But this isn't how to shift our minds.

Think of all the self-help books out there that promote strategies to feel more confident and happier. Often, they push strategies like mantras, affirmations, and confident body stances, or they encourage us to have conversations with aspects of ourselves to try to forcefully change our thoughts and feelings. Unfortunately, these techniques aren't sustainable. Instead, we have to confront the emotional realities of our past and present if we want to heal our thinking. This includes changing aspects of our life that don't work for us and making sure we get our deep emotional needs met. We also need support from emotionally aware people who can maintain a healthy and calm space for us to explore our true feelings.

As an example, let's say someone is suffering from a lot of self-hating thoughts. We can assume that this person must have come from a background where, either early on or later in life, they weren't given the love and support they needed from their family, peer group, or community. How can we be so bold in making this assumption? Because the mind always reflects real-time experiences in our life. Therefore, if we have self-hating thoughts, it means we must have been hated in a variety of ways or not given the love and care we needed. To heal these thoughts, the person must figure out what it looks like for them to be loved and seen on an emotional level. An effective mental health practitioner can provide insight to their emotional needs, and they can be a secure mirror for them, reflecting positive, real-time experiences that will eventually replace the old, hurtful ones. It's only through these corrective emotional experiences that their body can change how it thinks and feels.

The only way we can gain insight as to why we struggle with certain thoughts in our heads is by looking at our emotional experiences. Usually this requires getting help from someone else who is emotionally aware and who can hold a grounded space for us to explore our thoughts and feelings. This is because we're so locked into our automatic thinking and feeling patterns that it's almost impossible to see the forest for the trees on our own. It isn't until we give our body full credit for being a helpful and guiding force (and for never being random) that we can deepen our awareness and begin to heal.

The Body Communicates to Us via Thoughts, Feelings, and Physical Sensations

Our body speaks to us in a variety of ways, and everyone's relationship with their own system is unique. However, there are general rules that we can use to find clarity and structure.

Typically, our body communicates through our thoughts, feelings, and emotions, as well as physical sensations or ailments. Since it's highly intelligent, everything has a specific meaning, and everything is an attempt at having a conversation with us. Unfortunately, our culture and the western medical system tend to approach the body differently.

American culture puts high value on ideas like efficiency, productivity, power, control, and materialism, which don't promote deep listening to our body. Instead, we're taught to force our body to do what we want. This approach views the body as an inconvenience—something that breaks down and is inefficient and that gets in the way of what we're trying to achieve. We think of the body's natural functions as working against us, like an enemy, so we feel we must resist these functions in order to maintain our sense of control. This approach promotes a battle between us and our body, as if we can somehow live well while fighting in this way, which obviously isn't true.

Our body is not just our earthly vehicle—it is a manifestation and reflection of who we are including our energy, intentions, beliefs, and relationship with the world. Fighting against it only creates a self-hating cycle that causes us to experience pain. At some point, when our pain gets bad enough, we're forced to turn to a variety of medical interventions in order to survive, whether medications, injections, surgeries, or addictions. Even if we're "successful" at shutting the body down, it will never stop talking to us. Instead, it will just give us louder, more painful messages. Essentially, this is a battle we will never win, so it's in our best interest to build a wonderful, non-resistant relationship with our body.

We need help with listening to the body's messages because sometimes its communications are too big to confront on our own. Think of trauma, emotional pain, and stuck patterns.

Further, we all have a natural way of relating to ourselves that becomes so automatic that it's challenging to try to find clarity without help. We're the ones stuck in the middle of this storm, feeling the full blast of all our thoughts and feelings, so that puts us in the worst possible position to think clearly. It's way more efficient to be helped by someone else who can calmly hold space for us and see what our body is trying to show us. We must ask, "What is my body trying to tell me?" This is how we begin to build awareness and love ourselves. Like with any muscle that we use, practice helps us get better at listening to our body.

The Body Always Operates from True Reality

Our body is designed to always reflect true reality, so it will never buy into some new line of thinking that doesn't accurately reflect how we feel or what we've been through. It's only in dealing with the root emotional cause that our mind and feelings will shift naturally.

Our body is always fully present to the here and now, and it's a no-bullshit system. It can't be tricked into believing in something that isn't true for us. But how often are we trying to manipulate or control how our body feels, and how often do we believe we've gotten away with it? This is where we get ourselves into trouble.

Listening to the body takes courage because the information it gives us is always true and accurate. These messages are not always convenient or comfortable to hear because we may be asked to confront aspects of ourselves or our lives that need to change. But at the end of the day these messages are always here for our highest good.

Too often we try to disconnect from the truth by using our logical mind and making things seem more complicated than they really are. But our body always talks to us in simple and honest ways. Usually, we can break these messages down into basic categories of yes or no or gaining energy or losing energy. This might seem overly simplistic because life is endlessly complicated, but a lot of our decisions can be broken down this easily.

For example, say you've finally found a partner who is an extremely attractive and kind person. But your body keeps telling you they aren't quite right for you. How often do we doubt this feeling and say to ourselves, "Stop being so picky and just be grateful for them" or "I should be happy and thankful for this relationship"? If you were to listen to the guidance that this feeling is giving you, then you would have to confront the reality of leaving this relationship and trusting that someone else is out there who is a better fit for you. This is a very courageous task! Alternatively, if you don't listen and try to use your logical mind to remain in the relationship, you will slowly start losing your energy and lust for life.

Another example is someone who works at an extremely stressful job where they're mistreated, although they make a lot of money. I see this all the time in my practice. Usually, they have headaches or migraines every day, they're chronically fatigued, they can't sleep, they have no time for fun or travel, and their whole body is hurting as their stress slowly kills them. These are loud body symptoms that say, "What you're doing doesn't work!" But they have all sorts of reasons in their mind as to why they can't leave their job. They're too close to getting more stock in the company, they haven't been there long enough to go somewhere else, they just moved across the country for this job and don't want to give up now, and on and on. All of these logical reasons are there to resist the truth of their suffering.

Obviously, it isn't always easy to listen to what our body says and accept reality, which is often brutal and challenging. This is why we have these disconnecting mechanisms within us.

It takes incredible strength and courage to be present and to actively listen to what our body wants to tell us about our lives. This doesn't mean, of course, that we have to shift our life on a dime. Life has so many moving pieces that it isn't easy to do that. But we have to slowly practice finding the courage to take action based on our body's wisdom. It knows us better than we know ourselves, and listening is the only way we can live a truly good life.

When we're listening and operating within, we know what's true for us because we feel energetic, lighter, and more confident. Energy is our ultimate guide telling us how much we're listening to our body. I don't know about you, but eventually, I got tired of the fatigue that came with resisting the truth.

The body is a sage, our life guide, and our teacher. It's the most trustworthy tool we have. The practice is to find the courage to listen and see the truth.

The Body Is Always Oriented Towards the Healthiest Version of Ourselves

Our body is a highly accurate guide that is always leading us to become the most authentic, healthy version of who we are. And it has incredible awareness of how our life should look. This may seem hard to believe, as if the body has some future information about who we're meant to be, but our body has known from the start who we truly are and the life path we are supposed to take. It's empowering to give it this credit because it shows how magnificent and intelligent these earthly vehicles are.

How would your life be different if you always gave your body this level of credit? What awareness would you have access to? How would your relationship with your body change?

Some people struggle to be this open to trusting their body because they feel they've had past experiences where their body steered them wrong, or they've experienced harm. This is something women, people of color, and the LGBTQA+ community have experienced a lot. This is a tough situation to unwind and heal because there is, potentially, evidence that the body can't always be trusted. It's really important to heal these past traumatic experiences because without a trusting relationship with our body, we lose our best compass for life and end up disconnected from ourselves.

Our body isn't why these things happen to us, however. Our spirit specifically chose the body it believed would serve us the best in this life. Sometimes hurtful and harmful things do happen and other times we make mistakes. Part of this is just learning as we grow and other times it's because we live in a world where unjust things can happen. Shutting ourselves off from our body isn't the best way to process these experiences. Further, we need to forgive ourselves for not knowing any better when we make mistakes. The more we can heal and deepen our body awareness, the better we can navigate through life's complexities. The body knows how to direct us towards the life we are meant to live, and it knows the most efficient ways to help us heal. Listening to and trusting its guidance is critical for living a wonderful life. It took me a long time to realize this, to heal, and to live in an open and trusting way. There were moments when I felt like being open was a dangerous choice, but ultimately, I discovered how love and openness helps me live a higher quality life. I only came to this conclusion through amazing healers who held me with love and compassion and helped me realize, on a body level, that openness serves me better than being closed down.

The Body Only Shifts with Real-Time Evidence

Our body can't be convinced to change its conclusions about life and ourselves through logic and data. Our thoughts and feelings will only shift when we present our body with better, real-time evidence. What this means is that we need real experiences that register on an emotional level in order for the body to buy into a reality that could be different. Further, if we are trying to shift a longstanding emotional or mental pattern, we need repeated experiences over a long period of time to counter the overwhelming evidence of the past. This can be tough for people to understand because our culture promotes the power and use of logic, not feelings. We tend to believe that we can force our feelings and thoughts to change by just using our mind.

For example, take someone who believes their feelings aren't important and has learned to suppress them within their lifetime. Additionally, they have built an identity of someone who is easily liked and who takes care of the needs of others, and not their own. As a consequence of this imbalanced setup, depression and self-hating thoughts are expressed in their body. The overwhelming evidence that the body has experienced so far suggests that their value is only derived from being there for others and that nobody cares about them. No amount of logical thought can change this evidence. It's not until this person practices creating healthy boundaries and surrounds themselves with healthy people who want balanced relationships that they will be able to slowly change how they feel.

This process can be very uncomfortable, and to engage in it, courage and dedication are needed. This is because we are practicing new ways of existing in relationships with the people around us and with ourselves, and we feel vulnerable while trying to accumulate evidence that people will love us when we are being authentic. As long as we have the proper emotional support to engage in this process, we will see positive changes happen in our lives. This is how we truly shift the feelings and thoughts in our body.

Now, let's discuss the different ways our body communicates with us.

THE BODY'S CONVERSATIONS

There are so many unique ways our body can talk to us, and it takes time and practice to figure them out. These conversations are ongoing and have multiple levels, so we should periodically revisit our interpretations to see if there's more to learn. To start, though, here are some general ideas to help you notice your body's conversations in a clearer way.

Physical Conversations

On a physical level, a lot of the experiences we label as ailments or disease are actually our body giving us information. For example, headaches and migraines are often symptoms of unresolved emotional pain, resistance to truths about reality, an over- accumulation of stress, overwork, bad body posture, sitting too much, food allergies, exposure to mold or chemicals, or a lack of certain nutrients. These symptoms are just the tip of the iceberg of the possibilities, and a good practitioner can help you hone in on your body's specific messages.

In my practice, I have a lot of ongoing conversations with clients, encouraging them to try different things to see if they can get clarity as to what their body needs. But the ailments I mentioned in the previous paragraph are the most common I've found with people who suffer from headaches and migraines.

If we look at something a little more serious like fibromyalgia, which is unexplained body pain, we can ask interesting questions, such as, "What unresolved emotional pain or trauma is this person still carrying in their body?" and "What key emotional needs haven't been met for them, potentially for a lifetime?" Western medicine doesn't ask questions like this. It focuses on the physical level by evaluating nervous system dysfunction. But often, deep emotional pain is the true cause. It also makes sense to look at other factors like diet, exercise, exposure to toxins, and daily stress.

What about another ailment like chronic fatigue? We often lose energy when our life doesn't feel good for us or isn't aligned with what matters most to us. We may lose energy when our emotional needs go unmet for a long period of time or if we're living without love and care. Trauma and unprocessed emotional wounds can zap our energy and make us feel like we're carrying around an emotional weight that has become physical. Diet and medications can also play a role in the loss of energy. This holistic approach to medicine can open up a whole new way of thinking about our ailments and provide new possibilities to bring healing.

Cancer is tremendously scary for people, but the same interpretations apply. It's a disease in which the body attacks itself, and this can be reflective of someone's challenging relationship with themselves or their life. We can investigate unresolved emotional trauma and ask in what ways this person's life is not working for them or making them feel good. In what ways does this person fight against how they feel or who they are deep inside? It can also reflect an over-accumulation of toxins or unhealthy habits that is making the body sick. Or it can be a disconnection from joy, passion, or love. Any ailment or disease is multifaceted, and there's rarely one answer to solve it. But investigating in this way can shed light on the type of help we truly need.

Will listening deeply to your body cure cancer? I'm not claiming it will. I think there's a time and a place for western medical intervention and science. But I also believe that listening and becoming more aligned with who we truly are can bring incredible healing. Further, life isn't always explainable, and we can't always know why something is happening to us. But when we investigate with the assumption that our body is always trying to support our highest good, we can often experience deep, transformational shifts.

Emotional Conversations

Now, let's look at some examples of when our body talks to us on an emotional level. Let's start with someone who suffers from depression (something I know very well). This can be an indicator that many deep emotional needs in their life have gone unmet, including the need to feel seen or appreciated for who they are. This can also be an indicator that they aren't on their true life path, doing what matters to them, or not being in the right types of relationships. It could also be linked to hurtful and unjust experiences in their life, especially if they're part of a group that experiences discrimination, injustice, or racism.

Another common emotional symptom is anxiety, which is an indicator that a lot of emotional needs have been unmet. It can be linked to anxious attachment dynamics from childhood, close relationships that were unpredictable, and not fully connecting. This can cause deep insecurities and a feeling of being alone in the world. Anxiety is often linked to unjust or hurtful experiences, similar to the ones listed for depression, or not having the resources to get our basic needs met.

With the current insanity in our country, including gun violence, racism, hatred, and the spread of misinformation, anxiety is a normal indicator that the world is an unhealthy and unsafe place. The most effective way to soothe this type of anxiety is to be part of a conscious community of good people. This can feel counterintuitive when we'd rather hide in a corner and avoid the world, but love and connection are what help us feel better.

What about a feeling of unworthiness? Similar to depression, we can follow this feeling back through time and discover a lack of love, care, and understanding in our past (and often present). This stays with us, shaping how we think about ourselves and relate to others. Unworthiness is always a clue about painful experiences we've endured. In the healing process, these past experiences must be acknowledged and validated with care in order to understand the true pain that they caused. This will help to illuminate why we are currently struggling in the present moment. To fully heal, however, our body needs new experiences full of love, care, and tenderness to replace the old hurtful moments.

Our body will guide us to all of the truths we need to uncover in order to heal. Ultimately, all of our remedies for emotional pain will have something to do with getting the love and care we've always needed but didn't receive.

Mental Conversations

Western culture tends to think of the mind as something separate from the body, as if these two entities work against each other. This couldn't be further from the truth. Clearly, our brain is part of our body. Therefore, our mind, our body, and our thinking are part of the same system.

My first example about the mind comes from a personal struggle relating to fearful thoughts of becoming homeless. Before I found help to calmly hold space for these thoughts,

I judged them for making no sense because I come from an upper-middle-class family. I've always been provided for on a physical level without ever coming close to homelessness. But when I was working with a wonderful therapist several years ago, she made a comment to me during a session that made me see a connection to my emotional experiences. She told me that given my past experiences of emotional isolation, essentially having no one who understood my struggles in the ways I needed, I experienced "emotional homelessness."

The body doesn't distinguish between our emotional and physical realities. Oftentimes, what we experienced emotionally will be expressed in the physical body or as thoughts in our heads. This is why a holistic approach to the body allows for better insights as to why our suffering is happening. My therapist's comment helped me see the connection between my thinking and my feelings, which provided me with a new approach to evaluate my thoughts.

A second example comes from a client who has a lot of self-hating thoughts but comes from a great family. They feel their thoughts make no sense because all the evidence points to a "perfect" life. In order to understand why these thoughts were there, the client had to have the courage to see the deeper truths. They were never taught to track the emotional dynamics of their family system, so while their family seemed perfect on the surface, there was quite a bit of emotional dysfunction. As a result, this person's deep emotional needs weren't met. Remember that the mind reflects our emotional experiences, and self-hatred in our system is never random.

What's amazing about the mind is how quickly it will change if we give our body the things it's truly asking for. If someone with self-hating thoughts is given the acknowledgment and care they need for a long enough period of time, those thoughts will eventually go away. The amount of time their mind spends on the old, self-hating thoughts will decrease until they're no longer there.

My last example comes from another struggle I've had. For a long time, whenever I dated someone, I would become inundated by thoughts and images of them having sex with people from their past. Even if there was overwhelming evidence that they wanted me, the thoughts would still come, making me feel unwanted. It was horrible because it made me experience an untrue reality about someone I loved. From that place, it was hard to believe that my partner truly loved and chose me.

As I went through years of healing, I was able to see that so much of what I had experienced as a child was the feeling of being unwanted. These thoughts about my partner were a reflection of my past trauma. It was a way that my body was trying to heal my unresolved feelings. This was also a protective mechanism that my body used to try to keep me safe from being hurt again. Every time love showed up, it registered in my system as vulnerable and risky with the possibility of rejection. I still felt drawn to the partners who loved me, but a conscious effort was required to gather new evidence showing that my needs were being met. Having a good therapist really helped me to see this old mechanism and to understand that the true issues were not with mental projections about my partners, but with my past emotional experiences.

Spiritual Conversations

The last aspect of ourselves that we need to acknowledge is our spiritual needs and nature. Regardless of our beliefs, we all have spiritual needs that have to be met, just like any other need. We also have natural spiritual abilities that we must acknowledge and access if we want to live a fulfilling life. Again, our body is always in conversation with us about our spiritual needs, and it's our job to listen to how it's guiding us to get those needs met.

All humans are extremely intuitive creatures. There isn't a person in the world who doesn't have natural intuitive abilities—even those who believe they're logical rather than emotional people. And it's important for people who have honed in their intuitive abilities to keep an eye on their ego, especially if they have beliefs that they are more intuitive than the next person. This is incorrect. With the right support, anyone can enhance their ability to pick up information in ways that are unique to them. As with any other skill, we all have intuitive strengths and less practiced sides.

I put intuition in the spiritual category only to create some structure, but in practice, intuition is highly integrated into our physical, emotional, and mental levels. Therefore, it isn't separate from any other body system. I define intuition as the interpreter of the energy around us. This energy includes people's feelings and thoughts, how certain environments feel, our ongoing sense of how the Earth is doing, how our country is doing, the different spirits that are around us, and how aligned we feel to our life path. This information is expressed in a multitude of ways, but here are some examples to think about:

NIGHT DREAMS: Some people are extremely active dreamers, and their dream world is where they process their life experiences and learn things. We all dream each night, even if we don't remember our dreams, but acknowledging and working with them is a powerful way to glean more information about ourselves.

VISUALS: People who are clairvoyant can see a multitude of things in different moments, depending on who they are interacting with or the particular situation. This includes seeing different colors everywhere you go or around people, or having other visual experiences, including seeing things in your mind's eye. Visual experiences are often your higher self or your spiritual allies giving you insights or guiding you. When I am coaching people in my practice, I often have visuals in my mind's eye. This is a way that I am given information to support someone's healing journey.

AUDITORY EXPERIENCES: Have you ever sworn you heard someone say something to you, but no one was around or you were the only one to hear it? Or have you experienced hearing voices or new thoughts in your head in any situation. This can be a strong sense of hearing or clairaudience, which involves gaining insight from hearing things. To some, this may seem weird, but it's a real skill that some people can enhance by acknowledging and giving credit to what they hear that is out of the ordinary.

SMELL: This is one of my personal favorites because it's a sense that's very strong for me. Based on someone's smell, I can pick up an incredible amount of information, and I may also have visuals that accompany it. I use smells as a guidance system to see which emotions and memories are evoked in me, and in turn, I use this information as a mirror for what my clients may be going through. Our olfactory receptors are directly linked to the limbic system—the place where emotions are stimulated. Therefore, this skill, called clairalience, is a powerful way to tune into people. Another example is when we randomly smell someone's cologne or perfume, but no one else is around. This may be spirits or energies in the room with us.

TOUCH: Intuition is activated for some people through touching someone or something. Everything has an energy, so it makes sense that touching would be a way to feel that energy. Even on a basic level, have you ever had an experience when you held someone's hand or slept in someone's bed and felt emotions that you were sure weren't yours? This is an example of clairtangency.

TASTE: This one may seem a little strange, because how can someone taste information? But it definitely happens. Imagine touching an object or being near someone, and all of sudden, an unfamiliar or strong taste comes into your mouth. This is a taste that you usually don't experience, but you get a sense of what it means and why it's there. This is a version of how clairgustance works.

MENTAL VISIONS: Another strong sense arises for me when I sit with people in my office. I can hear voices, see images, or have new thoughts show up in my mind. Some might put this in the category of clairvoyance, but for me, it feels different—like new thoughts are being put in my head. I've learned over the years to distinguish between my own thoughts and internal voice and other people's, which allows me to discern if what I'm hearing comes from me or someone else. I use these mental insights as mirrors for what my client is going through or as wisdom that's given to me by my spirit guides.

BODY SENSE: I use body sense as one big category to organize information that comes through our emotions or physical body sensations. Some might call this clairsentience or clairempathy, but either way, it's about gathering information based on the feelings or physical sensations that show up in our body when around others. With body sense, it's important to practice distinguishing our own body sensations from what we pick up from others. We also must clear this information out of our system when we no longer want to feel it (there are a lot of ways to clear energy and many books that discuss this in more detail).

There are so many interesting possibilities for picking up information. It's only through acknowledging what we know to be true and building confidence in our intuitive senses that we get better at interpreting the energy around us.

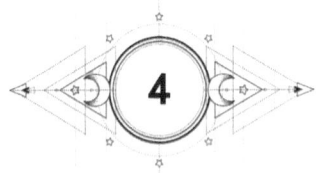

SPIRITUAL NEEDS

As spiritual beings, we all share the same core spiritual needs deep within. And like any other needs, in order to be happy and healthy, they must be addressed and met in ways that matter to us. The body is our guide, and it will tell us when we're aligned with these needs or not.

The first spiritual need is a sense of purpose, which brings motivation, passion, curiosity, and energy into our lives. This feeds us energetically and emotionally, and it's what helps us remain healthy and sane as we experience a world filled with trauma, hardships, and grief. Having a sense of purpose also helps us believe in who we are, why we're here, and what we can offer the world. It helps us build self-confidence and create a positive vision of ourselves. We all have unique gifts to offer, and as we bring those gifts forth into the world, we all benefit and the Earth heals. The opposite is also true: if we don't bring our gifts forward, the Earth gets sicker.

Some people may argue that believing in purpose only promotes an inflated ego. In some sense, this is true. We have to check in with our ego to make sure it isn't becoming too big. However, the ego is an important part of us that doesn't get the credit it deserves. Without the ego, we'd be incapable of thinking of ourselves as valuable and important—a key ingredient for emotional health. If we want a positive relationship with ourselves, we need to know and believe that we're valuable and unique in our own ways. We must also give the same value and credit to every other person on this planet, rather than thinking we are better or more special than anybody else. Nevertheless, without a healthy ego, we become disconnected from ourselves and our true offerings.

The second spiritual need is to connect to something greater than ourselves. There are infinite ways to do this, and it's important to believe in things that resonate deeply with our heart and soul. Some people follow religion, while others believe in the love of the universe or feel deeply connected to the Earth. Whatever your version may be, all that matters is that it's bigger than you and promotes the best version of your existence.

It should be a force or god to whom you can hand over all of your grief and baggage. It should also be a force that you can ask for help and support. In return, this presence should give you some form of love, care, and guidance. Love and care are my personal requirements for believing in something bigger than myself, as I believe love is at the center of the universe.

There are no rules as to who or what you believe in, and sometimes a combination works best. I personally feel deeply connected to the Divine Mother (my version of an unconditionally loving universe) and to Divine Mother Earth, plus I have a great list of loving entities that I'm able to call upon whenever I need them.

Even for people who are atheists, believing in something bigger is important. You don't have to believe in a god, but you can believe in things like the power of kindness, community, family, or science. This can be equally effective for bringing something big and important into your life.

There's a lot of evidence from around the world that this second need is very strong for us, given the universal proliferation of religions and spirituality in every culture. There isn't a place on Earth where people don't believe in something bigger than themselves, and it can be empowering and soothing to our body to have this relationship. If we don't take care of this need, there are usually consequences, such as depression, anxiety, and a disconnection from our life. In the worst cases, we might be susceptible to charismatic narcissists who claim to be a reincarnation of the divine or organizations who claim to be able to relieve our suffering in magical ways. People fall victim to this kind of influence when they're desperate to connect to something deeper or bigger.

Ultimately, it's our body that guides us to the unique versions of beliefs that are most aligned with who we are, and it's our body we should listen to when deciding what we believe in. Also, there are supportive teachers out there who can guide us to gain clarity about what our spiritual needs are and how we can get these needs met. These emotionally healthy teachers will always bring calmness, clarity, and energy into our body, and we should never settle for anyone who makes us feel unsettled, disempowered, or confused.

The third spiritual need is to be connected to love. Love is the answer to all of our problems and what we need in order to heal. Since we all come from a divine loving source, love is the most natural, intuitive state for all of us. It's what gives us the most energy and life force. Our body is designed to always aim us towards experiences that will bring us healthy forms of love. This is because love will always bring out the best version of us. Love is also self-generating and self-perpetuating. This means that it will never go away, and it has endless energy to show up in our lives.

Love comes in a million different forms, from the way our partner kisses us to meeting a kind person at the grocery store to spending time in the company of animals. But feeling loved isn't as straightforward as having a loving intention towards someone. Each of us needs to experience loving exchanges in ways that truly resonate with our body. We know when this happens because we feel full of energy, confidence, and happiness. We also know when someone tries their best to show us love but it doesn't make us feel better. Notice this difference and how the energy you feel in your body tells you accurately whether your needs are met or not.

As a general rule, we feel loved when someone truly tries to understand and support us in ways that matter to us. We also feel loved based on someone's internal intentions. For example, our body can tell the difference between someone who is trying their best but doesn't actually care about connecting with us versus someone who is trying their best and *does* genuinely want to connect with us. This is another example of how the energy never lies. Our body can always tell the difference. The challenge is to have the courage to express what actually makes us feel cared for and what doesn't. This way, the people around us will be able to learn how we feel and what we need. Plus, we have to be brave enough to surround ourselves with people who have the capacity to give us what we need and slowly let go of the people who can't or won't.

Unfortunately, in our current western culture, there are a lot of misleading ideas about what love is. On one end, certain belief systems are taught in religions like Christianity, which promote taking care of others before ourselves. This is talked about as a type of love, and in some contexts, that's true. However, too many people take care of others while never getting their own needs met. This formula isn't a recipe for success. Other ideas that try to promote love can be found in the self-help movement, including positive thinking, trying to always be kind, smiling more often, or listening well. In theory, these make sense, but in practice, the result is that a lot of people become disconnected from how they truly feel and what they truly need. At the end of the day, love isn't as simple as being kind and speaking in gentle tones.

Love is about authenticity, vulnerability, and intimacy. For example, we can experience deep love as we authentically express our feelings in a healthy way. We can also feel loved when we show up honestly with someone else, revealing to them how we're struggling with certain wounds. Love is a fluid system that is always changing depending on the situation. We have to be dedicated to checking in with our body about what we need and what the needs are of the people around us. This is how we feel the love that matters to us.

Another challenge with love is the trauma that comes with being human. It's a terrible initiation to come down to Earth from a source of love and have to experience the current state of humanity. All of us endure suffering and trauma of various kinds, although some are worse than others. This human initiation process is an important part of our spiritual understanding of the current problems, but it comes at a troubling cost. Most of us experience a disconnection from love for a certain amount of time as we dive deeper into the human dilemma. And although love never leaves our side, our perceived disconnection is very painful. At some point, through pain or suffering, we end up on a journey of healing to be reconnected to ourselves, to what matters to us, and to something bigger than us. It's this full circle that gives us the tools and insights we need to begin to offer our gifts to the world. All humans are courageous beings for attempting this learning process.

Believing in love is like being a warrior. We have to be strong to bring its energy into this world, and each time we bring more of it into our lives, the entire world benefits. Love is a powerful force that causes positive momentum in our lives. As we feel some of it, we crave more. And as we experience more of it, we feel better. Dedicating our life to experiencing real love and spreading it into the world is the ultimate purpose for all of us.

The last spiritual need is to be aligned to our life path. Similar to our life purpose, there's a path and a journey we all must follow to have the experiences we were meant to have on Earth. This path isn't easy, and it comes with many challenges, but also incredible rewards. Our body is deeply linked to our path, and it guides us along the way. It also brings us back in alignment with our path if we get lost. When we're aligned with our path, we have energy in our body each day. Alternatively, when we're off path, we lose energy.

Our path is designed to give us the experiences we need to grow into the best version of ourselves so that we can bring our gifts to the world. There are many body signs and symptoms to help us figure out what our path is, including our passions and what we are drawn too. Usually, it's our logic or our fears that get in the way and sometimes lead us to make choices that don't serve our best interests. The good news is that our body and the universe never give up on us, and we always have ample opportunity to correct our course. (Sometimes, a course correction is forced upon us.) These moments of realigning can feel very challenging, but they always happen for our highest good, even if in the moment, it feels like the whole universe is against us.

Another aspect of our path is "perfect timing." Too often, in our rushed western culture, we believe we're behind and won't get there on time. This couldn't be further from the truth. The things we're meant to experience are always waiting for us, and it's never too late. Plus, many of the transformations we're meant to experience take more time than we'd like. The universe has ways of cooking us, breaking us down, and helping us learn important lessons before allowing us to proceed. All of this is set up perfectly, so we just need to stay committed to our path and trust the perfect unfolding of our lives.

The ultimate beauty of our path is that we can't go wrong. It has a magnetic pull, and we're always drawn back into alignment. This is where we experience the most energy and lust for life. In this sense, there's nothing to fear, as long as we practice listening to what makes us feel the most aligned.

The importance of our spiritual needs is equal to that of our emotional and physical needs, and it's our job to tend to them all. A deeply satisfying spiritual life produces a wonderful version of ourselves existing in the world.

COVERT EMOTIONAL TRAUMA

When we hear about trauma, we tend to think about overt examples like abuse (physical, emotional, or sexual), bullying, or blatant examples of discrimination, hate, and violence. But we aren't usually taught to give credit to the harm caused by a whole other version of trauma called "covert emotional trauma." This is something that happens to most of us but is subtler and typically underneath the surface. I mentioned this type of injury earlier in the book, but now, let's define it and dive deeper into this very important and deeply hurtful sort of exchange.

We experience covert emotional trauma when we have small moments of hurt that happen to us thousands of times over the course of many years, perhaps even decades. These little moments accumulate into a large pile of evidence that shows us how much we're unloved, unvalued, or unseen, until one day, we reach a tipping point and have the body symptoms of someone who has experienced overt trauma. Think of the idea of dying from a thousand tiny paper cuts.

Covert emotional trauma is essentially a small exchange where love and care are withheld from us (consciously or unconsciously), or even worse, someone is thinking badly of us and trying to cause harm. We can tell this is happening based on the way our body feels and how we lose energy in these moments and feel worse about ourselves. Other emotional pains can get triggered after these exchanges, including depression, anxiety, and self-hating thoughts.

If we track what is happening in these moments, we can see that our body is picking up a very specific energy from the person, or persons, we are dealing with. The body notices this information based on someone's tone of voice, body posturing, and the ways they are looking at us while we interact. We can also notice this in the way someone talks about us or to us, moments where they invalidate our feelings or make us feel small or unimportant, or they are not able to meet our emotional needs.

Further, our body has the ability to understand how someone is truly feeling about us, and it knows the thoughts that are in someone's head. When people are thinking hurtful things about us, it creates a certain energy that is picked up by our body. This energy is just as hurtful, even if it's never vocalized.

Additionally, covert trauma happens because there is no attempt to repair the hurt that is caused. This can be due to someone's inability to be emotionally close with us, their lack of emotional awareness, their unwillingness to make us feel loved, or a mixture of many reasons. Also, we play a role if we don't attempt to vocalize the hurt feelings we are having.

Covert trauma is much harder to notice because it happens under the surface. Our body feels its impact, but we can't always spot it in the moment. As a result, we often struggle to validate and give credit to how hurtful and damaging these moments truly are.

In the beginning of emotional healing and awareness-building, we need someone else to validate these harmful moments for us, because, at first, we doubt their importance. We might have thoughts like "Maybe I'm crazy" or "Maybe I'm making too big of a deal out of this" or "I'm being too sensitive and should just let the little things go." Often, the unhealthy people in our lives have said things like this to us in order to discredit our body's information and have us doubt our own feelings. We end up having very little confidence to trust how we feel, which is why we need someone else to inject confidence back into our system. The truth is that we've all been hurt in small ways that deserve to be acknowledged, especially if we are trying to heal.

Additionally, these hurtful moments in any of our relationships deserve to be addressed, especially the exchanges that stick in our minds and negatively impact the dynamic. Usually, the healthy people in our lives are more than happy to repair moments that may have hurt us. A universal healthy standard is that all of our feelings matter, whether big or small, and anyone who invalidates our small feelings without a willingness to repair the relationship might be unhealthy for us. Whenever we feel hurt by someone, we deserve a healthy space to express those feelings and be heard. This is a big part of how healthy relationships function.

Another healthy standard for relationships is that good quality people in our lives tend to participate in making the dynamic feel emotionally safe and filled with love. And since these people care about our feelings and wellbeing, they want to know when we feel hurt by them so that they can repair it. Of course, we aren't always given this kind of healthy space. How often has someone refused to hear your feelings and instead said something like "Can't you ever let things go?" or "You're always so sensitive" or "I never said that"? There are endless ways that we can be invalidated. Often, it's a form of gaslighting that causes us to doubt how we feel or disregard our feelings. But we always have a right to our feelings, no matter what they are.

Another factor with regard to covert emotional trauma is that the external dynamics don't always match the internal ones. As I've said, emotional dynamics may look great on the surface but feel entirely different on an internal emotional level. Here's an example:

> Client A is a 24-year-old woman who struggles with self-confidence, social anxiety, and getting her needs met. She tends to be stuck in a pattern of always trying to please people. She has a harsh inner dialogue, but she believes she comes from a great family who loves her. Her parents both express how much they love her and how proud they are of her. They've always supported her life choices and they show her lots of affection. Therefore, she thinks she was just born with these internal emotional struggles.
>
> Her father is very charismatic and hilarious. He entertains the family with crazy stories and opinions. However, over the course of our time together, I learn that her father has a large presence and dominates conversations to the point that no one else can get more than a few words said before he's off telling his next story. He also tends to compete with people for attention, always one-upping stories or turning other peoples' stories into tales about himself. He's very emotional and takes things personally when someone expresses their feelings of hurt or frustration towards him. Meanwhile, her mother is quiet, has a small presence, and doesn't stand up to her husband, even when he's out of line.

Essentially, client A has had her feelings minimized or dismissed her entire life and was never taught that her feelings are just as important as her father's or anyone else's. Her body symptoms tell this story. The complication came from the fact that her parents are good people who love her very much, but that doesn't excuse the lack of space and attention towards her.

In healing this, we had to validate the goodness of her parents while giving credit to the true emotional problems within the family dynamic—that her father was consumed by his own feelings and her mother didn't take up enough space or stand up to him. This is one example of how the external doesn't always match the internal.

Remember, too, that your body always knows the true dynamic and emotional exchanges in any environment at any moment. Don't forget to ask yourself such questions as, Do I gain or lose energy when I interact with this person? Do I feel more anxious or depressed? Do I feel like a bigger or smaller version of myself? Do I feel confident, calmer, and more secure? Do I have more self-hating thoughts? Contemplating these questions gives you simple techniques for checking in with yourself and building consciousness in your daily interactions. As a general rule, anytime you feel better in some way, you've almost certainly had a healthy exchange.

Lastly, covert emotional trauma stems from a narcissistic root, so if you have this invisible trauma, you probably come from a narcissistic family dynamic. This doesn't mean that your caretakers were or are bad people, but in any narcissistic setup, our emotional needs won't be deemed as important as the other person's.

Covert emotional trauma is a very real experience that many people go through. If you suffer from emotional pain that "can't be explained," it might be a true experience for you, too.

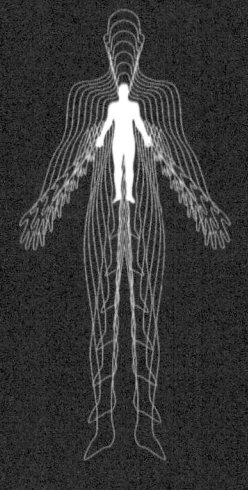

SECTION 2

TAKING ACTION

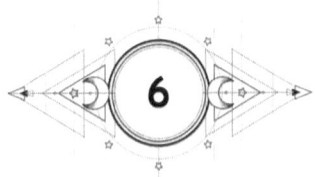

IT ALL STARTS WITH OUR DREAMS

Every one of us has unique gifts that need to be manifested in the world. They're meant to be given to others so that the world can heal and get better. You may not know yet what your gifts are, but everyone has them. In fact, these treasures are so important to healing the world that our life should be built around making them a reality. True happiness comes from discovering and offering our gifts to others.

Our gifts are a unique expression of our spirit, ways in which we want to contribute love and positive evolution to humanity and the world. Each of us is designed to contribute many loving gifts to the Earth, and often these gifts can be found in our strengths and passions. Another way we discover our gifts is through the challenges that we must overcome.

Our gifts are also linked to our life dreams. From a body level, we feel our life dreams as deep cravings and longings—symptoms of a primary need that always calls us. Like with other primary needs, such as love, we can experience various pleasant body symptoms once we take action to fulfill these deep needs and bring our gifts into the world. Such body symptoms include increased energy, happiness, inner peace, passion, and inspiration. Our body is a vessel for carrying our gifts into the physical world, and it knows how to guide us to make them happen.

When we talk about our gifts, however, it's important to keep our ego out of it. Otherwise, we might judge someone else's gifts as better or worse than ours. The size of our contributions is irrelevant. What matters is feeling aligned with ourselves. Our gifts will always have a positive ripple effect, so we don't need to worry about how big they are. Each of our contributions is unique to us. There's no one else on the planet who can offer your gift exactly the way you can. Trust your body and how it guides you because it will never steer you wrong.

A couple of years ago I heard an amazing story about a grocery store bagger who wasn't particularly fast but whose checkout lines were always the longest. The people working at the grocery store were really struck by this because in this busy day and age, you would expect shoppers to be in a rush. What was so special about being in his line? It turned out that he wrote kind notes and put them in the customers' bags. It touched so many people's hearts that they went back for more.

This story proves the point that no act is too small. Everything is a contribution to healing this world and our hearts. It's fascinating that this person was drawn to embrace this unique act, which most of us might overlook as too simple. Clearly, he was able to trust his body, and it guided him to one of his gifts for the world.

There are many ways to discover our gifts. Sometimes, we overthink them, even though they're right in front of our eyes. This is because we're trained to always compare ourselves to everyone else, thinking that something "big and shiny" is better than what feels right.

One person's life gift might be to spread kindness through how they interact with people in their everyday life. For someone else, it might be to surf a 100-foot wave. Both of these are of equal value because what matters most is that they're aligned with what the person feels called to do, and it fills their soul to do it. Everyone's gifts to the world are amazing and very much needed!

A great way to start figuring out your gifts is by getting clear about your life dreams. These dreams are our biggest cravings for the kind of life we want to create. Our gifts and dreams are linked together, and often, it's through pursuing our dreams that we discover our gifts.

Discovering Your Dreams

If you close your eyes for a few minutes and allow yourself to envision the most satisfying version of your life, what do you see in your mind's eye? Most of us struggle to let go and allow ourselves to dream big, or authentically, because we bump into our logical mind that tells us it could never happen. We're told that as adults we need to be responsible, realistic, and "successful," that we need to make something of our lives, and that we shouldn't waste our time acting like children, pretending that magical things can happen. But yes, let us pretend! Let's be completely unreasonable and unrealistic for a little bit. Let's have fun and bring back our inner child.

Have you ever noticed how kids aren't afraid to dream big? They want to be the president, become an astronaut, or cure world hunger. This is because they are still connected to the loving source that we are all a part of, and they know that this source will help them create anything. It's the adult world that eventually puts doubt into this awareness and takes those dreams from them. What a terribly harmful act! Why has squashing dreams become a normal and common thing in our western culture? It's time to heal this devastating theft, both for our kids' sake and ourselves.

The first step to discovering our gifts and building an amazing life is to create in our mind the most incredible life we could ever imagine. If you are not used to dreaming, it can take time to give yourself full permission to get big and be joyfully creative. How big are you willing to dream? How authentic to your true self are you willing to be? The body always knows who you truly are and who you are meant to become. The trick to this process is to always be in full conversation with your body; to let it guide you to awaken to what matters most to you.

As you begin this process, be aware of all the distracting things in this world, both superficial and egoic. A lot of people get trapped into thinking that their dream is to be a millionaire, to have a perfect body, or to become famous. But a lot of the time, these ideas are driven by ego and wanting to be better than others. And they have nothing to do with being aligned with our gifts or greatest good.

Our body can help us tell the difference between what matters and what doesn't. When we dream of something that truly matters to us, we instantly become alive and gain energy because our true dreams are life-giving.

Another way to distinguish ego from truth is to notice when we are feeling hyperactive, ungrounded energy. This type of energy is a key symptom of the ego because our true needs and dreams will always make us feel grounded. Begin to pay attention to these energetic differences and see if you can notice the difference between your ego and your true self.

Also, in dreaming big, don't overlook your *basic* needs. It's perfectly healthy to want a good house, a comfortable salary, and a kind partner who loves you. These things are practically a requirement for going after larger dreams because often our basic needs have to be met before we can be open to other experiences. But while aiming for a good house, notice the difference between wanting a mansion (ego) versus a safe and healthy place to live.

Let's practice stepping away from the superficial and put more value on quality. It's in these distinctions that our intentions can really shine.

That being said, there's no limit to how big you can dream, and most of us are aware of ideas that have been in our hearts for quite a long time. Vocalizing these past and present desires can breathe new life into ideas that we compartmentalized a long time ago. It's time to take these gifts off the shelf, dust them off, and start thinking about how you can bring them into existence.

Even if you have no idea how to make your dreams come true, don't let that hold you back. We don't have to know how to manifest what we want—that is the universe's job. Our job is to have faith and confidence that if we believe our dreams can happen, and if we are always pursuing these desires, the universe will take care of the rest.

Last, I recommend getting a *dream journal*—something you can carry with you and write in as ideas come up. I always carry my journal with me in my work bag, and I continuously add to it. I also write down ideas, personal feelings, and messages I receive from my spirit guides. It's useful to make our thoughts and feelings concrete by writing them down. This helps to bring our ideas into the world. So, before you read any further, find something you can write in.

Life Dream Exercise

With your journal by your side, close your eyes, and imagine a life where you could do anything and everything you've ever wanted. Imagine that you live in a place that calls to you, that you have a home you love with a family or community that truly supports you, and that you have an abundance of money to pay your bills and provide for yourself and your loved ones. Imagine what the healthiest and truest version of yourself would look and feel like. Imagine that you have the power to positively change the world in any way you want. What kind of life do you envision? What gifts do you want to bring into this world to make it better? And what life experiences have you always been called to or been curious about?

Really step into this vision and soak up the happiness, energy, and peaceful feelings that it should give you. Make sure to include every little detail like the smell of the woods or the sea, the smile on someone's face, or the satisfaction you feel in your body as you do what you love. What is your perfect life?

Spend at least 10 minutes visualizing and feeling this version of your perfect life. This may sound like a long time, but it takes time to settle into this new reality. Also, this is a listening exercise, so spend some time checking in with your higher self (and your body) to see how you are guided. Be open to whatever process you need to go through in order to truly connect to your dreams and life goals.

Sometimes, it can be helpful to spend time revisiting your younger self, both when you were a kid and when you were an adolescent or young adult. Remember what those versions of yourself loved about life or what you were drawn to. What dreams and hopes did you have back then? What brought you pleasure and joy?

Also, notice if you bump into any mental blocks during this exercise, such as parts of you that resist the joy of having dreams. Be tender with these parts, and remind yourself that this is just a dream space. This is meant to be fun, and you don't need to worry about reality here. Enjoy yourself!

As you do this exercise, notice anything that brings you energy and makes you excited about life. Write those ideas and images down in your dream journal, and notice what happens after writing them down. Sometimes it can help us access a very exciting and creative space.

Spend time doing this exercise every day for a week. If there are people in your life who will do the exercise with you, do it as a group. This can be very powerful! And notice how your visions slightly change each time you do this practice.

Keeping detailed notes about your dreams is a very powerful first step to bringing your visions into reality. Once written, feel free to express your dreams in whatever ways suit you the best. If you are artistic or visual, paint your dreams and create vision boards. If you are musical, play your dreams. What matters is that they fit who you are authentically. The more expressive you are on the physical level, the quicker these dreams can come to fruition.

Visualizing our dreams may seem quite basic, but it's incredibly challenging. As we engage in this process, we are actively going against our western upbringing and belief systems. However, dreaming is a deep way of loving ourselves, and it allows us to step away from outside influences that have tried to make us inauthentic.

Last, embracing our dreams takes time, so go easy on yourself. If you struggle with creating and visualizing your dreams, don't force yourself. Just remain open and keep participating in the exercise each day. We never know how long it will take to unlock our authentic and creative nature. Sometimes it can help to keep a question or two active in your mind each day. I keep post-its on my computer or refrigerator with questions that I want answers to, and I allow the answers to slowly reveal themselves in the coming weeks or months. By remaining open, you will gain the insight you're looking for. It's only a matter of time. Here is a question you can start with: "When I was young, what brought me joy or what was interesting to me?" Notice what pops into your mind as you keep this question active.

Our Life Challenges Can Reveal Our Gifts

Another way to become clear about our gifts and life purpose is to give credit to the challenging and painful things we've experienced. We tend to misinterpret why these struggles happened to us, thinking it was some form of karma or punishment. However, it's often these challenging aspects of our lives that are the training grounds for us to gain the awareness we need in order to provide our gifts to the world. Once this training is complete, a rewarding yearning to help others can be activated.

For example, my personal struggle with depression, anxiety, and an aggressive inner dialogue has allowed me to become a very deep and compassionate person with a plethora of emotional tools to help others heal their emotional pain. I didn't know it at the time, but my emotional struggles were a training in the healing arts. As I started to heal myself, a craving to help others who struggled with the same issues arose.

Another example comes from a client of mine who has been in a number of physically and emotionally abusive relationships over the course of her life. These dynamics have been incredibly painful for her to go through. But as she started healing and taking action to bring healthy love back into her life, she began to have a calling to be a social worker and help other victims of domestic violence. Her personal experiences have made her an incredible healer with a big heart.

Our pain and struggles are often a way for us to bring our gifts into the world. As you practice visualizing your dreams, spend time reflecting on the challenges you've faced throughout your life to see if more clarity about your gifts unfolds.

Finding the Gold

Once you have a clear vision of your life dreams, and if you are committed to manifesting these in the world, you'll next need to sort through your ideas and figure out what calls to you the loudest. Use your body as the best gauge for this exercise because you will feel an increase in energy and excitement when you engage with the dreams that you need to pursue first. Most of us have multiple dreams that want to be manifested, however, it's important to organize your cravings and find structure with what needs to happen first.

It's also very important to be witnessed during this process, so if you have a healthy person in your life who supports your dreams, ask them to help you find clarity. Oftentimes we can struggle with allowing our dreams to be big and with giving ourselves the permission to create a life that truly means something to us. It can also be hard to have clarity about what to pursue first or how to do it. It's with the help of our supportive people that we can build a plan and gain confidence to start moving in the right direction.

After inviting someone you trust to be part of your process, read out loud to them the visions that came through to you while doing the dream exercises and what you long to create for yourself or the world. Include anything for which you have true passion and any past memories of what used to bring you joy. Also, check in to see if you feel underconfident or stuck in pursuing your dreams. What blockages are there for you? Share all of this until you feel complete in your body. Being witnessed in this way is a powerful practice of manifestation.

Next, ask for their helpful feedback. What did they notice about you when you were sharing? What struck them in particular? What thoughts and feelings showed up in their mind and body as they witnessed your dreams? What clarifying questions do they have for you? And last, make sure they check in with you by asking "How can I be supportive of you in this moment?"

Allow for as much time and conversation as is needed in order to have full clarity and understanding around your dreams and what you are interested in manifesting. Sometimes this can take a couple of days and sometimes it can take a couple of months. This is not supposed to be a rushed process; rather, an exciting journey!

Next, see if you can work together to come up with practical first steps to start this journey. What are the first couple of steps that you can do right now? So much of this process is about the accumulation of little steps over a longer period of time that allows us to get to our goals. If we do too much, too soon, the process can become overwhelming, and we can shut down and give up. Notice whether you have judgements about the little steps, as if you aren't doing enough. Be kind to this part of you and challenge yourself to be slow and intentional with moving forward.

Once you have clarity about your dream and some initial steps you can take to move in the right direction, create a goal for yourself that you are willing to commit to. What actions are you committing to take and in what time period? What challenges are you willing to confront in order to grow? And in what ways are you willing to be held accountable to what you promise to do? Ask your partner to help you gain clarity with these commitments if you feel stuck in anyway. You should come up with no more than three commitments.

Ceremony

A powerful way that we can manifest new energy in our life is by using ritual. Before moving forward, think about how you would like to create a ceremony around your commitments. This doesn't have to be super-complicated, but we want to create a space that is special and that honors our higher self. You will also need at least one person to witness you in this ceremony, so invite them to be a part of it. One example is to light a candle and say something to begin your ceremony like "I am here to make commitments to accomplishing my life dreams and I call in sacred and supportive energy to be with me now. Please be here with me and help me manifest my dreams. And so it is, amen."

Having your written commitments with you, say them out loud for at least one person to witness. Use the phrase "I am committed to ...."

Next, ask your person to hold you accountable to the commitments you are making in the moment. Example phrases are "Please hold me accountable to my commitments" and "Please help me to accomplish my goals."

Last, post your commitments in a place you easily see every day, somewhere in your living space. Make sure to designate a couple of minutes each day to read your commitments out loud so as to keep this energy active and alive.

Finally, think of a way to end your ceremony. For example, thank your witness for being a part of this process and then speak out loud your gratitude for the opportunity to engage in your life in a conscious way. I also like the phrase "May everything I've committed to today come true and be done for my highest good. And so it is, amen." Then blow out your candle.

There are no "right" ways to create a ceremony. It is a creative process that is supposed to feel exciting and energizing. So, design one that truly works for you!

LIFE DREAM WORKSHEET

First, answer the following questions on a separate sheet of paper. Then, for each set of questions, spend time connecting to different parts of yourself. This can be done as a form of meditation, whether sitting quietly or walking. Invite these parts in, connect to them, and ask for their help in answering the questions.

1. When you were a little kid, what did you want to be when you grew up? What things fascinated and interested you? What brought you joy?

2. When you were an adolescent, what things were interesting or stimulating to you? What passions did you have and what brought you joy?

3. As an adult, what things do you find interesting? What stimulates you? What passions do you have and what brings you joy?

4. Are there any life experiences you long to have? What is it about these particular experiences that makes you feel drawn to them?

5. What painful and challenging experiences have you been through in your lifetime?

6. How have these challenging experiences changed you in positive ways?

7. What important tools and awareness have you learned through these challenges? Do you have any desire to share these tools or awareness with others?

8. What aspects of growing up in your culture, and in the world, do you dislike and wish to see change? What do you notice around you as being unfair, unjust, and unhealthy?

9. If you could positively change the world in any way you see fit, what would you change and how would you do it?

10. If you could successfully create and accomplish anything you wanted, what would you do and why?

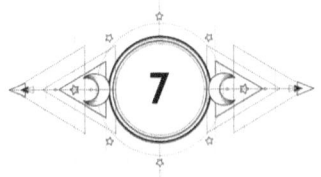

THE POWER OF MANIFESTATION

There are many skills and abilities that are unique to being human, but one that isn't given the credit it deserves is our power to manifest things out of thin air. A lot of books have been written on this topic, and we have movies like *The Secret*. However, many of these resources are geared towards manifesting material, superficial things that promote our ego. It isn't as common to talk about this skill with regard to creating a life that's more aligned with our true self and bringing our gifts to the world. Certainly, I don't recall coming across any directive to use our body to figure out what we truly need.

It's crazy when we begin to notice this incredible power that we all have to bring things into form. Our cravings for creating are not only part of our human DNA, but they also come from intentions we set before we come to Earth. In essence, we've committed to bringing new awareness into this world that triggers healing and growth for ourselves and others. We've also committed to bringing in new technology that helps the human species to evolve in positive and healthy ways.

Our ability to create has vastly accelerated in the past century and we've become so accustomed to the advancement of technology that we forget that all of this is possible due to the incredible power of our minds.

Our minds are like 3D printers, taking a mental visualization or intention and manipulating physical reality to make it real. In this regard, we're skilled energetic beings who have a serious influence on the energetic level of everything around us. This skill is so powerful that all we need to do is aim our intentions at what we want, and it will eventually appear right before our eyes. Unfortunately, we haven't been taught how to use this tool appropriately, so most people who know how to use it get caught up in greed and power.

While this is a mental power that we all have, the process of creating is actually very intuitive on a full body level. Clearly, the mind is part of the body, so it makes sense that manifestation is a full body process. A lot of great inventions started out as a body intuition and then slowly manifested into form. This is why a lot of "aha" moments happen when someone walks away from trying to figure something out logically. The breakthrough might happen in the shower, when they aren't thinking about it.

After we set our mind on something we want, we must listen to how our body guides us towards the right opportunities to make it happen. Our body is deeply connected to the energies all around us, and when we set an intention, there's an energetic rippling effect that spreads outward, shifting those energies. The universe adapts to the intentions that we create, and our body knows how to track this energy. It's deeply linked to the universal energy, and it guides us to the right opportunities to manifest our desires into form.

As we become clear about the wonderful life we want and the gifts we're meant to bring into the world, we need to turn to this manifesting skill to bring our cravings into reality. This process is a combination of setting intentions, listening to our body, listening to the universe, and having the courage to take small steps forward.

Manifestation isn't just about bringing things onto the physical plane, however. It's also about how the journey of creating changes us. The universe helps us become the person we need to be so that our energy can match the intentions we've set. For example, after feeling frustrated with unsatisfying relationships over and over, I eventually set a very strong intention to bring a healthy and loving partnership into my life. I did this without knowing what chain of events I was putting into motion, and without even considering that at the time I could never have handled a loving partner. What ended up happening was a series of uncomfortable events that brought about emotional healing. It helped me grow into the person I needed to become to match my intention.

As we go down this intentional path, our body gives us the usual indicators of being aligned (gaining or maintaining our energy), but if we stray from the path, we start to lose energy or experience emotional symptoms. We must use how we feel and the energy in our body as a guide to determine whether our intentions are aligned with our highest good from moment to moment. No one is perfect, so we all stray from our path at times. But as long as we stay as attuned as possible to our body, we will always know when we're in need of making adjustments.

This process of manifestation is like any other muscle: the more we use it, the better our skill will become. Many entrepreneurs, for example, have a lot of practice with this skill, which allows them to repeatedly create what they want.

For many of us, it can be difficult to accept that we have this much power to create. You'd think this would be one of the first things we'd learn as kids because it's so natural to who we are. Plus, it would be super helpful to know how to use it properly. But since this isn't the case, you may find yourself thinking thoughts like "I'm not God. I can't do these things." But the crazy thing is that you absolutely can! All it takes is setting proper intentions and letting your body guide you through the journey.

One thing to note is that many people think they must first build confidence before they can take action and create. Society misleads us, saying that we must first believe in ourselves, but this is a trap. Confidence is never built ahead of time. It's only through accomplishing things and gathering evidence about our abilities that confidence is slowly built. So, in this regard, we have to take action while we feel under-confident. Otherwise, we'll never move forward. This is another reason why it can be so helpful to have someone else give us hope and encouragement to be our best self.

Intention-Setting

In order to manifest what we want and need, we have to be very clear and direct in our intentions. Visualizing and speaking our intentions out loud every day, followed by the appropriate action, are what will bring our thoughts into form. The trick is being incredibly direct in what we want, which most people struggle to be.

Especially in our largely Christian-based culture, many people bump up against feeling selfish when they ask for exactly what they want. They have thoughts like "How dare I ask for so much! Shouldn't I just be happy with what I already have?" or "I'm asking for too much. I shouldn't be so selfish." We have to notice this cultural training and confront these beliefs as old ideas that don't serve our best interests. Nothing is bad about becoming the best and fullest version of who we are.

Our intentions should revolve around our short-term and long-term dreams and life goals, as well as the actions that need to happen to make those dreams become reality. Figuring out how to create the right intentions is a body-based practice that requires trial and error. We start by trying our best to write down the intention we think we need, and then try it on for size. We say it out loud and see how it lands in our body.

If we say exactly what we need and want, we'll feel empowered, energized, and grounded in our body. If our intention isn't quite right, our body will feel off in some way. Then, we'll know that our intention needs to be reworked. Again, support can help us in this process because healthy people will give us the right permission to go big with our intentions. This can turn an intention from "I would like a better job where I'm valued more" to "I want a job where I get paid my value, which is six figures, and where people see and value my skills in creating curriculum and leadership." We then repeat this process with each of our dreams until we have a full list of detailed intentions. There's no limit to what we can ask for, and our lists can be long. But ultimately, we must check all of our intentions against how our body feels. As long as our body says we're still in alignment with what we need, we're good to go.

As you write your list, notice when your body gives you a feeling of completeness. This is when you know that no more intentions are needed for now. My daily intention list, which I know by heart, has about 30 intentions. I'm always adding and subtracting from it as my body instructs me.

There are no rules about your intentions or the order in which they must be spoken. Try saying them out loud and see which ones your body indicates should go first, and so on. Certain intentions may not feel right on a particular day, so you may want to put those aside until you feel like you need them. This is an intuitive and fluid process.

Most of us have a few intentions that are deeply important to us, and as we say them out loud, we calm down. It can be nice to start with those to help you feel settled and grounded at the beginning of your daily intention-setting. I have anxiety around money and my business, so I say those intentions first because it's soothing for my mind and body.

Another element of structure that I find to be helpful in manifesting is making sure our intentions are addressed towards a bigger force and asking for help in the creation process. This doesn't need to be religious or even spiritual if that doesn't feel right to you, but our intentions need to be aimed at something. And it's extremely powerful to ask for help from a force bigger than ourselves. There are a million ways to do this, so be creative and do what feels best for you.

As an experiment, try asking for help out loud right now and see how your body feels afterwards. You can use this as your template if you need one: "Dear Universe, please support me in creating the life I've always dreamed of, and help me bring my gifts into this world." Repeat this out loud a couple of times so you can really get a sense of the energy it creates. How did it feel in your body when you asked for help? It should feel good and energizing, which is why we know we must do it. Now imagine what it would feel like if you asked for help in manifesting all the things you need!

The last thing to address with intention-setting is to make sure you do it every day or close to every day. Each morning is a new beginning, a clean slate, and you need to set up the energy of the day so that it unfolds in the way you need and want. I understand that we all have a lot of responsibilities, so setting intentions isn't always a priority. I recommend having a short intention-setting list and a longer one, as well. On the days when you don't have much time, at least say the short list out loud.

Since I have two young kids, most of my morning prayers and intentions are said in the car on the way to work, in the car on the way to drop them off at school, or in the shower. This is fine. The intentions will still work! Saying them out loud is the most important part.

Setting intentions and manifesting our reality takes time and dedication, and we never know for sure what we're ultimately going to receive. In this regard, we have to be patient and allow it all to unfold as it's supposed to. I find that the universe tends to provide a version that's even better than I could ever imagine. So trust is a big part of this process, knowing that whatever comes to pass will be for our greatest good.

Below are a few of my daily intentions, some of which I've used for years. You can use these as a reference for directness and for expanding the possibilities of what you can ask for:

1. Dear Divine Mother and all of the good, true, and beautiful spirits who are here with me today: Please continue to help me have an overabundance of money and resources that always flows into my life and practice at all times, with ease and grace, so that I can always pay our bills on time, provide a comfortable and easy living for myself and my family, and keep my family safe and healthy. Please help me continue to always have these resources so that I can focus on being a great husband, great father, great healer, and kind human.

2. Dear Divine Mother, please continue to help me have an endless supply of new clients who flow into my life and my practice at all times, with ease and grace, so that I never have to worry about finding clients ever again. Please remind my old clients of my value, and return them to my schedule if they're in need of my work.

3. Dear Divine Mother, please watch over me and my family today, and please keep everyone safe and out of harm's

way. Please protect my family and keep my family healthy and strong. Please return my kids to our house today safe and sound.

Universal Listening

After we set our clear intentions and begin the practice of saying them out loud each day, it's time to deepen our relationship with the universe (or whatever big force we're speaking to). The universe is the big life force all around us, and it constantly interacts with us and guides us as we move through our life. Like our body, it has our highest interest at heart and is a trustworthy guide for finding our path and manifesting our dreams. It's intricately linked to our body, and it constantly feeds our body vital information and guidance. Just like any other relationship, we can build a stronger and deeper bond with the universe as we spend more time interacting with it. It's our partner in co-creating reality, so after setting our intentions, our job is to "let go and let God (universe)," as we notice how the universe guides us into manifestation.

This is a fascinating process because after we set our intentions, we have no idea what journey we've started or the process we must go through in order to have our dreams become reality. In this regard, we have to put all of our trust and faith in the universe's ability to help us reach our goals. Therefore, we must listen for when the universe directs us towards action. Learning how to notice this universal language is crucial for successful intention-setting, goal completion, and creating an aligned life.

One common challenge with universal listening is getting caught up in our head and overthinking the process. We might worry that we'll miss an important sign from the universe. In response to this fear, we become hypervigilant and overanalyze everything around us. We end up stuck in anxious thinking with thoughts like "Was this a sign? Maybe it was! How do I know if it was a sign? Am I overthinking it? Maybe it wasn't a sign." This just leads to confusion and feeling lost. We might also disregard signs if they seem too mundane or small, but important signs may very well be small. Universal signs aren't always visual either. They can be new awareness that just shows up in the body. Regardless of how the universe talks to us, our body is always the best gauge for recognizing messages. Also, we can set intentions with the universe to only give us signs that are clear and obvious to soothe our worries.

One way to notice signs is to look for things that are outside of our daily rhythms and patterns. They're moments that evoke curiosity, interest, excitement, weirdness, or new ideas. You might have a thought like, "Hmm, that's weird" or "Hmm, that's interesting" or "Whoa, what are the chances?" These are great moments to notice as potential messages. It might be something like a comment said in passing by a coworker that triggers something in you, giving you ideas. For people who are active dreamers, messages can sometimes come through at night. A sign can also be as simple as a craving in the body to go do something.

Regardless of signs, we should always come back to whether we gain or lose energy in our body. When we experience an authentic moment of guidance or help from the universe, we will always gain energy and feel grounded. Conversely, if we are overthinking it and trying to create signs out of nothing, we will feel less energy, less grounded, and more chaotic.

Once you experience something that you feel is a message, guidance, or confirmation from the universe, write it down and keep track of it so that you don't lose it. You should have a running list of potential actions to take, ideas that you need to consider, and inspirations. These will help you move closer to your dreams and gifts.

The whole goal of this listening process is to inspire creative ideas and then to take courageous action in order to test which ideas work. The universe continuously provides us with the inspiration and creative ideas we need in order to gain clarity as to how to best manifest our dreams. It also provides us with the right people and opportunities to get the job done.

Remember that we're meant to become different people as we set intentions to manifest our dreams and be fully aligned with our path. In this regard, we have to go through certain experiences that change us. We don't always account for this being part of how the universe is guiding us. All we can do is practice trusting that the universe and our body know all the experiences we are meant to go through in order to manifest our dreams. Additionally, the universe will provide confirmation along the way that we're aligned with our path and doing a great job.

As we engage in a daily practice of universal listening, we become conscious co-creators of our life. Saying our daily intentions in the morning is part of this process, and it sets up the energy for the day. Additionally, it gives us the proper lens through which to view our life. For example, if one of my intentions is to have the universe provide clear and obvious guidance for me today, I will be more inclined to notice the signs as they arise. Also, I am co-creating with the universe with regard to how it can best communicate with me.

As this process unfolds each day, I accumulate awareness from the universe on the steps or ideas I should attempt next to manifest my intentions. I use my body to intuitively decide which of these inspirations I should act upon first. This is a trial-and-error process mixed with body listening and intuition. As I engage in this process more, it becomes easier and I gain the clarity I need to bring my intentions into form.

When I was first attempting to manifest a thriving acupuncture and coaching practice, I had a dry erase board in my apartment on which I wrote the ideas, guidance, and opportunities that came to me each day. This became a huge list! It included people I felt drawn to meet, things I needed to update on my website, random things I heard in conversations, and random thoughts about where I could attract more clients. I used my body to sort through the entire list (about 50 items), asking it to tell me which ideas I should implement first. I would choose the ones that caught my attention or gave me energy. I spent about three years going through almost that entire list, while adding new items to it along the way. This was a much longer timeframe than I had originally thought it would take. It also took time for me to find the courage to engage in some actions, and I had a lot of anxiety for the first two and a half years. But eventually, it all started to come together, and I've had a thriving practice for the past seven years. This process was transformational for me, and it created a confidence within me that I never thought I would have. This confidence allows me to stand firm in my authenticity and to pursue bigger ideas—like writing this book! Looking back now, I can see how much I needed to change as part of the process, which took time. But the universe and my body always knew that.

At first, most of us feel under-confident about our ability to recognize messages from the universe, which is normal. This is another reason why it's advantageous to have someone support us in the process and help us build confidence. Also, since manifesting can take time, we need supportive people to help prevent us from becoming discouraged. They can help us maintain the drive and persistence we need to keep chipping away at this process.

One of the biggest lessons I learned from my manifesting journey is that showing up and not giving up is 80% of the work.

This takes serious courage! But if we have enough trust and determination, we can create anything.

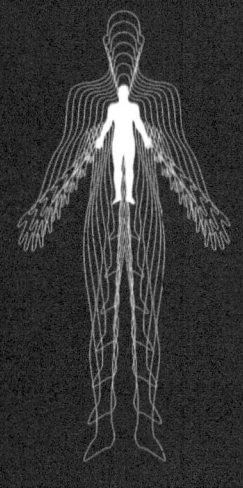

CREATING HEALTHY DYNAMICS

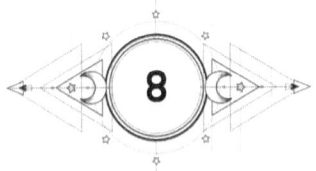

UNIVERSAL HEALTHY STANDARDS

As we learn to listen better to both our body and the universe, we also need to have a set of healthy standards—universal rules and ideas to build our life around. We use these standards as a lens through which we view the world. They help us remain clear-headed about what we should expect in relationships and in life. This is crucial, because our lives are endlessly complicated, and it's easy to get lost when trying to determine what's good for us. Once we have a good grip on what's healthy, these standards become an anchor and a filtering system for us.

First, we need a reference for what healthy exchanges and healthy relationships look and sound like. Healthy people have access to a certain amount of love and care, both for themselves and for others. This comes partly from having lived experiences, but also from a willingness to self-reflect, grow, and be open to connections with others. Healthy people understand that life is imperfect and that we all struggle and make mistakes. They also tend to be willing to own their imperfections and mistakes, rather than projecting their emotions or blame onto others. Lastly, they have a value system based on kindness and love for themselves, others, and the world. This isn't to say that healthy people are perfect. We all struggle with many personal flaws and life challenges, but healthy people put in the work to grow, heal their mistakes, and become better versions of themselves.

When you're in a relationship with a healthy person, there's usually access to empathy, warmth, and care. Not only do you feel connected to the person, but you also feel understood without judgment. These are people you can go to for comfort when you're struggling with life or when you aren't at your best. They will hold a grounded space of love and support for you. Alternatively, you can go to them in moments when you're excited or feeling playful. They will enter into this energy with you as well. In these relationships, you can make requests for your needs to be met, and these people will be willing to put energy towards helping you feel good in the ways that matter to you. Also, you can vocalize your boundaries with healthy people, and they will be likely to respect your wishes.

It doesn't take much experience to become clear that we're much more comfortable in our body when we're in a dynamic with healthy people. These relationships have a dramatic, calming effect on our nervous system. Our mind stops racing, our insecurities are soothed, and we feel more confident about who we are. We begin to believe that our authentic self is valuable and worthy of love because, finally, we have the evidence. These dynamics can kickstart our creativity and passion. Once we have a reference for the positive impact of a healthy relationship, we can filter unhealthy people out of our lives. It becomes obvious who they are and how bad they make us feel about ourselves.

As we upgrade our standards for the healthy interactions we deserve, we become empowered to test out who is good for us and who is not. We make clear choices about who we allow into our lives. We get a clear sense of who is healthy for us by setting boundaries, requesting needs, showing up more authentically, engaging in moments of vulnerability, and navigating conflict.

Depending on the response we get from these interactions, we gain clarity about the dynamics of the relationship. If we are dealing with a healthy person, then we will end up with good signals in our bodies.

It can take time to have enough evidence to decipher who is healthy for us and who is not. It's only by continuously engaging in our relationships in healthy ways that we eventually gain insight. For instance, when we set a boundary, which can be as basic as saying, "No, this doesn't work for me," healthy people respect our feelings because they want us to feel safe and good. Unhealthy people, on the other hand, might have a big emotional reaction in these moments. Another example is requesting a need like, "It would really help me feel more connected to you if you'd hold my hand more often when we're in public. Is that something you would be willing to do?" Healthy people want us to feel good and will respond positively to these requests or at least engage in a fair compromise that works for both people. On the other hand, unhealthy people are likely to become defensive or turned off to our requests.

The same healthy standards can be applied to other environments like work or community groups. We deserve to be in healthy spaces, and our body symptoms can help us test the dynamics. For example, how we're treated when we ask for something we need at work, or if we set a boundary, will tell us a lot. Is our good standing with our boss threatened? Do we lose favor in these situations? Based on the feedback we receive, we can design a plan to change our life for the better.

There are many challenges that come with practicing healthy standards. First, we can discover quickly that there are close people in our lives who are quite toxic for us. It can be very hard to walk away from these relationships, and there may be family or community consequences when we try to do so. Second, we may have other needs that are higher priorities than healthy relationships. For example, some people are terrified of being alone and would rather be with someone who isn't healthy than by themselves. Third, if we have a belief system that tells us we aren't worthy of healthy relationships, it can be challenging to accept a higher standard with regard to what we deserve, especially if we're surrounded by toxic people who assert that we have no value.

In the beginning of practicing healthy standards, it might feel like a leap of faith to believe that healthy people even exist. It may feel like we're taking a huge risk of losing all of our relationships, even though they're unhealthy. If you feel this way, be patient with yourself as you seek experiences with healthier dynamics.

These ideas can also be applied to how we approach spirituality and religion. Often, we're taught to have toxic and unhealthy relationships with the divine. We might have been told we're sinners, that our presence in the universe is insignificant, that it's selfish to ask for too much, or that we need to be punished in order to live a humble life. This couldn't be further from the truth. Our healthy standards should absolutely be upheld when it comes to our spirituality, and the bigger forces we are interacting with should always be unconditionally loving and hold us with understanding, kindness, and care. This doesn't mean that painful things won't happen to us, but the dynamic with the divine should be one where our experiences are always for our highest good; and through which we experience deep life lessons that help us grow and expand our awareness about love. If we can build healthy relationships with mere humans, we should expect to be able to do the same with an all-knowing universal force.

At the end of the day, building our lives around healthy standards and healthy relationships is crucial if we want to create a satisfying and secure life. It's the only way to bring out the best version of ourselves, and it's the only way to open to the fullness of our creativity, passion, depth, and understanding. As a bonus, when we move through the world as a great version of ourselves, it gives permission to others to find healthy versions of themselves too.

Creating Emotional Security

After we have a clearer sense of what healthy relationships are meant to look and feel like, we can create dynamics with emotional stability and security. Not all healthy relationships offer the same amount of emotional security, however. Every relationship is unique in what it brings to the table, but as long as we enter into a healthy dynamic, we can practice accepting whatever limitations we come across.

Emotional security comes in many forms. On a basic level, it comes from healthy relationships with people who love us for who we are. To the best of their ability, these people support us in becoming a great version of ourself and living a fulfilling life. Even if some of these people don't fully understand us, and can't meet us at deeper emotional levels, they can still be healthy presences in our life. So, don't be too quick to turn away from people simply because they are limited in what they can offer us.

Too often, we have unfair expectations that someone who truly loves us should be able to meet our every need. Or we have the mistaken belief that our romantic partners should be the ones who understand us on the deepest level. While our long-term partners will definitely get to know us in more intimate ways than most, they are oftentimes not the people who can hold deep emotional space for us. And this doesn't mean that they're the wrong partner. It just means that this isn't their role in our life. Sometimes, it's people that are further removed from our lives and our baggage that have the most capacity to help us go deeper within ourselves—perhaps a therapist or key friends. So many people in this world don't even have a basic level of emotional security in their lives, so we must acknowledge that it's a big deal when we have people who support us in healthy ways, whether perfect or not.

A deeper form of emotional security comes from being in a dynamic with someone who can validate and understand what we're experiencing on a physical, emotional, mental, or spiritual level. These are people who have been through it themselves or people who are actively choosing to grow and better themselves. As a result, they have the empathy and emotional capacity to meet us on the levels we need. We know when we come across someone like this because our body tells us. We feel a deep sense of inner calmness, deep validation, a big boost of confidence, energy, happiness, a desire for closeness, or a craving to go deeper within ourselves. It's almost as if our body and spirit are recharged. We all need at least one of these people in our lives if we are going to heal. This may seem far-fetched if you've never experienced it before, but these dynamics do exist, and it's our job to be open to finding them.

There are two moments in my life that stick out as being of equal impact—moments where I received deep emotional security and validation on a level I'd never experienced before. The first time was during one of the early meetings of a group I joined called "Practicing Living in the Moment," when the leader, Warren, opened up about his struggle with alcoholism, jealousy, personal insecurities, and a challenging inner dialogue. I was shocked because I'd never heard anyone express this level of vulnerability before, and no one had ever validated my suffering in that way. For the first time, I realized that I wasn't alone in the world, and I started to think that maybe something wasn't wrong with me after all. I also started to be aware that my painful struggles were less personal than I had ever realized. As I listened to Warren share, a blissful and very light feeling poured over my body like water, as if I'd taken ecstasy and fallen into some dream world full of love and happiness. It was the most incredible relief I'd ever experienced up to that point.

These were unique body symptoms for me because I was dealing with such loud depression at that time. I always felt so heavy in my body, and I never seemed to have access to lightness or happiness. But in that moment, there was an endless supply of it that I could tap into. The moment lasted all of two minutes, but it fundamentally shifted me. It opened something up within me and started to change my thinking.

The second moment happened when I was sitting in my therapist's office years later. It was a therapist who seemed to understand my struggles and who held a powerful and supportive space for me to heal. I don't remember the exact conversation with her, but I expressed a painful thought that I was suffering from. The response I received from her, both in her words and her body language, was so validating and understanding that I felt extremely seen in that moment. This was so rare for me. A deep relaxation and relief immediately came over my body to the point that I craved a long nap on her couch. I knew that if I was allowed to nap, it would be the most restful sleep of my life. I remember thinking, "Oh! So this is what it feels like to be relaxed!" It showed me it was possible to have inner peace while still alive.

The body symptoms of deep emotional security are so fantastic and healing that it's impossible to miss these moments when they happen to us. The symptoms come in many different forms, both loud and quiet, but the bottom line is that they help us feel calmer and better.

Each of us needs a big dose of emotional security and validation in order to recover from the damage caused by the loneliness and trauma that we've been through. Absorbing this emotional nourishment takes time, and we need to be given repetitive doses of it in order to heal.

When I first started going to therapy, I thought I would be healed within three months and then be good to go. But every time I went, I uncovered more issues, and my awareness grew. Between sessions, I also had trouble holding onto the awareness I had received; within two days, the awareness and relief I'd felt during therapy was nowhere to be found. At the same time, I was in the healthiest relationship of my life (with Sashya), who was giving me so much love and validation in the ways I needed. With all of this love and weekly therapy appointments, it still took me almost three years to recover. And that's just the starter dose. We all need ongoing support and love throughout our lives to continue to go deeper within ourselves and remain connected to who we are and what we're here to do.

To bring in relationships that provide us this type of emotional security, we must wake up to the truth that we are very dependent on others. This isn't because we've somehow failed at life or that we're not strong enough to be independent. It's that we are a connection-based species, and we can only thrive when we are in close connection with others. This is human nature. Therefore, it all starts with our ability to be open to bringing quality people into our lives. We must create space and opportunities for these relationships to find us. Often, this shift in mindset is enough to start creating a whole new life, one that is deeply satisfying.

The Power of Vulnerability

In the past decade or so, people have begun to wake up to the true power of vulnerability, especially if you follow key authors like Brené Brown, who talks a lot about it. Being vulnerable in healthy and appropriate ways can bring us huge advantages. On the one hand, it can help us see the healthy people around us clearly and determine whether we're in healthy environments. It can also allow us to get more of our important needs met in our various relationships. And it gives us access to more natural energy and passion about life as we live more authentically. Vulnerability is an amazing force that takes strength and courage, but the payoffs are immense. Once we get a dose of how good we feel when we're vulnerable and met with love, there's no turning back.

In this harsh world we live in, the idea of being vulnerable may seem crazy. In theory, it opens us up to all sorts of pain and disappointment. If this is the case, then why be vulnerable? The truth is that vulnerability is the only real way to create the deep connections and intimacy that we need to feel loved and fulfilled.

When we're born, we're very vulnerable creatures, not just because we depend on others to survive but because we instinctively know that it's the way to connect. And connection is one of our deepest needs and sources of emotional nourishment. But as we grow and experience the trauma of living, we naturally close ourselves off in stages to form a protective barrier. This may seem like a logical response to pain, and it does protect us for a certain amount of time but, ultimately, it makes us feel alone. It prevents us from connecting on a deeper emotional level with others, which, ironically, is what we actually need to feel safe. It's a terrible feedback loop that most of us have created unconsciously.

As our suffering grows due to a lack of connection with others, we're eventually forced to reevaluate this unconscious choice and investigate whether openness really is the way to live. The difference this time is that we're healthier adults with emotional support, so we can see the possibility of being open and safe at the same time. This is how I approach vulnerability in my work with my clients. I help them feel safe as they choose the right moments to open up and connect.

When you think back on your life, can you remember times when you made unfortunate choices to be open to people or experiences that weren't healthy or safe for you? As a result, you were hurt.

This often happens when we're younger because without enough life experience, we inevitably trust the wrong people or situations. These experiences can leave an indelible mark on our psyche and lead us to distrust everyone. How often do we think of these past wounds when we consider being vulnerable with someone in the present?

The good news is that there's a big difference between being vulnerable with unhealthy people versus healthy ones. Making this distinction is crucial to feeling safe: we must be vulnerable with the right people.

Before we talk about the process of opening up, however, we first need to define what it means to be vulnerable with others. It's all about building quality connections by revealing parts of ourselves. In this way, vulnerability is linked to authenticity, intimacy, and honesty.

On a physical level, we can be vulnerable with people when we share close space or share our physical body with them. This tends to be the most obvious type of experience people think about when they try to understand vulnerability. On an emotional level, we connect with others by revealing who we are authentically, which includes our life passions, quirks, imperfections, flaws, needs, fears, and struggles.

For example, as I mentioned earlier, I have a long history of struggling with depression and anxiety. For most of my life I tried my hardest to hide this from my romantic partners, but it never led me to have satisfying relationships. However, when I met my wife, I decided to take a courageous leap and not hide my authentic struggles from her. This was very hard for me. I was afraid she wouldn't be interested in me anymore once she found out who I was. But I had to reveal these parts of myself if I wanted to know her true feelings for me, and it ended up bringing us closer. Now I know that she actually loves me for me. That's what vulnerably with the right people tends to do.

Another version of being vulnerable on an emotional level is being honest with someone about how we feel, especially about behaviors and dynamics that don't feel good for us. Sometimes, this involves setting healthy boundaries within relationships. Other times, it means directly requesting that our needs be met. Regardless of what we share, the conversation is likely to be positive if the other person wants us to feel both good and safe.

On a mental level, we might reveal our inner dialogue to others—the thoughts that cause us to suffer or the inspirations and ideas in our heads.

On a spiritual level, sharing our spiritual beliefs and experiences can be a very important way to build intimacy.

As you begin to practice being vulnerable with others, it's all about baby steps—key moments when you reveal a little bit of yourself in order to test the waters, see how you feel, and discover the reaction you receive. Your body is always the best gauge of this. Initially, there has to be some good body indicator that the person you are attempting to be vulnerable with is healthy for you. This can be as simple as feeling calm around them. Once you have some indicators, find a moment in conversation to share a truth about yourself. It doesn't have to be a huge reveal at first.

For instance, a good place to start might be telling a friend that you've been struggling during the week with a lot of anxiety about your job. Or you might tell someone you've just started dating that you're a very affectionate person and want to be in a relationship with someone who enjoys affection. The responses you receive from showing up more authentically will begin to let you know if the other person is healthy for you.

This process takes time, both for us to get comfortable revealing ourselves and also for the other person to become comfortable with us. Everyone deserves many chances to show up well in our life. So even if you don't get the response you were hoping for right from the start, give kind feedback about what didn't work for you, and ask for a different response the next time. This is a great way to see if you're connecting with someone who wants to grow and better themselves.

Additionally, getting a great response from someone doesn't mean it's enough evidence to confirm that they're a good person for you. Again, give yourself many chances to have positive inter-actions with someone before concluding who they are. This is the only way to keep yourself safe and vulnerable at the same time. Too often, we go too fast with someone who makes us feel good because we crave that level of connection so much. This is normal, but we all need to rein ourselves in and pace ourselves while enjoying the gifts of good people.

As we accumulate positive experiences and feel good vibes from these interactions, we begin to see the true power of vul-nerability. With the right support and practice, we can build our entire life with vulnerability at the center of it along with other important things. Who wouldn't want to have a life full of deep, meaningful connections where they can be loved for who they truly are?

Vulnerability is a lifetime practice that always takes some level of courage, but it does get easier over time. In some moments, it may feel like work, but it has a wonderfully positive effect on our life and is one of the main components to a happy and healthy life. It's never too late to try it, so start today!

THE REPETITIVE NATURE OF
REASSURANCE AND HEALING

O nce we have found some healthy relationships and practiced being vulnerable, we have a greater ability to heal deeper parts of ourselves. This happens naturally as we get more of our needs met, such as being loved and cared for in the ways that matter to us. As this loving energy enters our body, however, it causes a natural dissonance that triggers our unresolved thoughts, feelings, and wounds to arise—the ones that still prevent us from believing we deserve to be loved for who we are. This happens because loving energy exists at a higher frequency than the energy of hurtful thoughts and feelings. This loving energy starts to reattune us to the loving beings we truly are.

But detoxifying old patterns is uncomfortable, and it takes time to cleanse these old beliefs from our system. It's equivalent to shining a very bright light on someone who's been in a dark space for a long time. Their natural response might be to turn away from it, as though it's bad. It's not until they have the capacity to adapt to the brightness that they can reemerge and be comfortable living in the light. There are many parts of us that have been left in the dark for too long, and we must be patient with them as they adjust to the light of love.

The idea that love detoxifies and triggers us may come as a surprise, especially if you've bought into the misleading notions of love that we're shown in the media. Our culture teaches us that when true love enters our life, we simply open up and embrace it easily. But that isn't the way it is for the average person, and it's not what love is designed to do for us.

These misleading ideas can be very hurtful to people who are uncomfortable with love. They might think something's wrong with them because they can't give over to love automatically. The reality is that love is a fierce force of nature that we underestimate when we only think of it as gentle and tender. Although these aspects of love do exist and are real, there's a whole other side that's fierce and brutal, and we need it to heal. How often do we go through a hard life challenge and come out the other side transformed in ways that are positive and helpful? This is the real power of love. It kicks our ass in the ways we deeply need, even if we're totally unaware of it. We must remember this aspect of love and realize that it's also a part of being in healthy relationships.

When I first met Sashya, I had been working very hard to heal myself for several years. About a month before I met her, I had a big mental shift and realized that a key attribute I needed from a partner was gentleness and kindness. This may sound basic, but my emotional trauma had made me forget how gentle I was, and I was typically drawn to women who were harsh, emotionally cold, and distant. But when I remembered my own gentleness, it opened me up energetically in a way that allowed me to spot my wife. She is an amazingly loving and kind person, and I was really struck by her during our first interaction.

About four dates later, I had a crazy moment. I was standing in my kitchen getting ready to meet her, and all of a sudden,

I had the realization that she was the person I wanted to be with long-term. That feeling was a first for me. And then, a loud internal voice said, "Are you sure you're ready for this? This is going to be really rough." The feelings that came along with the voice were loving, and I realized I was about to enter into some difficult healing and growth. Interestingly enough, it didn't scare me because on an intuitive level I already knew what I was getting myself into.

Sure enough, being with my wife, who unconditionally loves and supports me, triggered so much of my baggage that I immediately entered into therapy to help me process it all. I was bombarded daily by a super negative inner dialogue accompanied by anxiety, depression, and a loud inclination to flee the relationship. Thankfully I had the strength and mental resilience to face my baggage head on, combined with weekly therapy sessions. It took me about three years of intense work to finally confront and process all of the wounds (although working on ourselves is a lifetime commitment and never ends!). And I will admit that during that time, I struggled to see that love was at the root of my healing. But now that I am through it, I'm so grateful for the way love challenged me to heal and grow. It has allowed me to make huge gains in my personal growth, emotional healing, and awareness. This is the true power of love and healthy relationships.

Strategies for Working with Our Triggers

Any close relationship we are a part of will always offer us opportunities to learn about our emotional operating system and the wounds we carry. When our wounds get activated, we are triggered into old emotional patterns. Ultimately, it's understanding these triggers that gives us access to healing our wounds. The good news is that healthy relationships not only trigger us, but they also give us access to a lot of help and support.

One thing we need to be clear on when it comes to healing is that we need others in order to heal. This is a function of how vital quality connections are to our nervous systems and our overall wellbeing. Additionally, we have to be willing to ask the healthy people in our lives for help because that's one of the reasons why they're there. In asking for help, we can reduce our suffering dramatically. If you struggle asking for help, remind yourself of how good it feels to care for somebody you love when they come to you in a time of need. In healthy dynamics, we should gain energy by providing care for others because this builds close, intimate bonds. The same goes for how it feels for them to take care of us. Ultimately, we work together as a team with the supportive people in our lives to help heal each other.

When it comes to dealing with the triggers that arise within our relationships, knowing what to ask for and what to do in those moments can be incredibly helpful for navigating your baggage. Here are a few strategies to consider.

The first strategy has to do with our insecurities and needing repetitive reassurance. Being in a close relationship is very vulnerable and will usually activate a lot of our insecurities. Oftentimes, we project these insecurities onto the people we love or we suffer with the insecurities internally. However, the most efficient way to end our suffering, and to grow, is to actively utilize our healthy relationships by repetitively seeking out reassurance. At a core level, all humans need continuous reassurance if they want to have a long-lasting feeling of confidence and security. As long as it's done in healthy ways, getting reassurance will exponentially speed up our emotional healing. Additionally, good people in our lives will always be more than happy to support us and offer reassurance because it feels good to reassure the people we love.

The main insecurity that was activated for me in my relationship was the fear that Sashya would leave me for someone else. In reality, there was never an ounce of evidence of this, but the insecurity made it feel very real in my body. The first thing I had to do when this wound got triggered was to evaluate the projection and come back to reality: "Does Sashya want someone else? Can I find evidence of this?" For me, the answer was an obvious "no," but this logic didn't typically soothe my body.

When first unwinding an emotional wound, the projections are so visceral that we need real-time evidence to counteract them, not logic. The easiest way to get real-time evidence, which was very hard for me at the time, was to go to Sashya and ask her directly. "Babe, I'm struggling with this insecurity that you would rather be with someone else and not me. Is this true?"

She always responded, "No, of course I don't want anyone else but you." If the response feels authentic, which in her case it always did, it will instantly catapult us back into reality and we will gain instant relief. This would usually be followed by a loving hug, which is something that enhances how much love enters my body.

This process of gaining repetitive, real-time proof takes time. This is nothing to be ashamed of because it's a normal part of the healing process and being in a healthy relationship. Plus, it creates the deeper level of intimacy we desperately want and need. It's a humbling process to openly admit that we need support for our insecurities, but it comes with huge rewards when we engage in this work with good quality people.

It took about three years of being vulnerable with Sashya in our marriage, and hundreds of moments when I asked her to help me return to reality, for my wounds to heal. Even to this day, seven years later, I still have moments when I say, "Babe, you still want me and no one else, right?" She quickly helps me resolve this insecurity.

The second strategy relates to pacing ourselves as we get used to closer levels of connection and intimacy. As we enter into healthy relationships with people who actually want us, it can feel overwhelming and smothering or cause anxiety. This is because we aren't used to this level of love and connection. Despite these challenging symptoms, these aren't signs that the relationship is bad for you. In fact, it's the opposite. Your body tolerance for love may be low, which is why you feel overwhelmed.

Many of us have been forced to live without enough love for way too long, and we have forgotten how much we crave intimacy on a deep level. In order to be successful in bringing more love into our lives, we have to find the right pace to keep our nervous system regulated so that we don't shut down, self-sabotage, and run away.

For instance, if you have a wonderful friend who wants to hang out all the time, you can ask in a loving manner for some space and time to yourself. Make sure to be explicit in why you are requesting this. It's not because you don't love hanging out with them, you just need time to recharge. Or if you keep having intense and deep conversations, you can request doing something together that's light, silly, and fun. This will allow your time together to become more sustainable for you. These strategies will also work with people you're dating.

With a romantic partner, you may want to make a request with regard to sex and touch that help you stay regulated and open to them. For example, I sometimes make requests to slow down during sex, which allows me to take some breaths and calm my overactive mind so that I can stay present. You may also want to take breaks during sexual exchanges and focus on staying connected and present together. All of this allows you to remain present and keep showing up in love, even when it's hard to do.

Another strategy for building up tolerance for close connection is to engage in structured practices that deliberately make you go deeper. Many activities provide this, but two of my favorites are deliberate, long hugs and committing time for eye-to-eye connection. Long hugs with someone you trust are wonderful and challenging. I recommend setting a timer and starting with five minutes, working your way up to ten minutes. By using a timer, you won't have to preoccupy your mind with how much time has passed. Make sure to hold each other for the entire time.

What's interesting about this practice is that you go on a journey of different experiences in just five minutes. It starts out nice and easy. Then, as you progress past the social norm for hugging time, you begin to feel natural discomfort. Your mind might start to race as you think about what the hell you should be doing during this hug because you're just standing there holding each other. If you can take some breaths and make it past the mind-racing moments, you might enter into a calming space where your nervous system feels better and you breathe easier. You'll begin to see that closeness can be a nourishing tool. If standing for this long is too hard, try your hug lying down (aka cuddling).

Eye-to-eye connection is another version of this practice. You can do it sitting face-to-face, about a foot or two across from someone you trust. You can also do this while lying in bed, looking at each other. Take a few breaths together while closing your eyes so that you can get centered in your body before connecting. Once you feel grounded, open your eyes and stare into your partner's eyes. Allow yourself to be open to whatever happens next. Usually, the beginning is the most challenging. Our discomforts, anxieties, and insecurities get triggered, and we want to close our eyes and turn away. See if you can notice whatever gets triggered, and simply invite it in without fighting it. Focus on breathing as a way to keep you grounded. It's okay to smile and laugh with each other as well. If you need to look away for a second to re-center, do so, but then reconnect. As you stay with the connection, something will inevitably shift, and you'll probably start to feel calmer. This is the intimacy coming into your body and nourishing you. Keep focusing on your breath as this happens, and enjoy the comfort you feel. Usually all of this happens in waves of discomfort moving into comfort and back to discomfort again. Be aware of this and stay with the eye-to-eye contact for as long as you agreed upon. When the alarm rings, or whenever you feel complete, thank your partner and disengage while staying in some form of connection with them. This is a great time to reflect and talk about your experience.

Ultimately, having intimate connections with others is all about slowing down. This isn't easy for most of us in our fast-paced world. But the intimacy we crave can only be found in being, not doing. This is how we find the nourishment we crave.

The last strategy, as I mentioned before, is to get support from a therapist, coach, friend, parent, or someone else outside of the relationship. It just needs to be with someone who is emotionally conscious and who can hold a grounded and kind space for us as we work through our issues. I would never have been able to make it this far without counseling. I had two different therapists for the first three years of my marriage, and two years later we did couples counseling for more than a year. It was tremendously helpful to me and our partnership. It allowed me to grow and heal in ways that I was never able to do before. Additionally, going to a therapist really helped me to regulate my nervous system which is one reason why therapy can be so effective. It allows us to get out of panic and come back to reality. Once we are back in the present, it's easier to see that we are safe and that love isn't scary.

MEETING OTHERS' NEEDS AND HANDLING CONFLICTS

Besides getting our own deep needs met, we also have to meet the needs of the people we care about. This is part of what creates a healthy and satisfying relationship, one that can last a long time. To clarify, this doesn't mean that we will be the source of meeting every one of their needs—that would be imbalanced, and it's impossible. However, for the people we love, there should be a natural drive to take care of them in whatever ways feel healthy for us.

Although we all have similar needs to be loved, cared for, and closely connected, we're also different from each other in so many ways. It takes time and effort to understand what it means to care for someone in the ways that matter to *them* because it requires that we step into their version of the world and let go of our own. We're all guilty of making assumptions about what our loved ones want from us without checking in with them. And we typically make assumptions about their needs through the lens of our own past experiences and what works for us. However, if we are trying to be effective in loving others, we have to be willing to open ourselves up to the endless varieties of what love looks likes and what actually feels good to them. This can be quite a challenge, especially for our egos. But at the end of the day, we have to ask ourselves one question: "Do I want my loved ones to truly feel loved by me?"

The following are some strategies for being there for others in ways that matter.

The first strategy is to simply ask directly what they need from you and be open to what they request. This doesn't mean you have to do something that crosses any of your own boundaries, and it doesn't mean you have to sacrifice for someone else in an unhealthy way. But beyond this, how open can you be to someone else's needs? You can ask what's important to them and what makes them feel like you love and care in the ways they need. Not everyone is used to being asked about their needs so directly, let alone getting any of their needs met. We need to give space and time for people to reflect on this.

Also, this level of directness can be overwhelming for some, and for them it may not be the most effective strategy. Alternatively, consider a brainstorming session together to gain clarity. Oftentimes, our closest people have many insights to share about what our needs may be because they are our best witnesses. Working together to gain clarity can be a fun way to bond and grow.

I'm also a big fan of trial and error as long as we don't take it too seriously. What better way to explore your loved one's needs than trying something out and seeing if it works for them. This should be fun and playful.

The second strategy is being open and willing to participate in someone else's passions and interests. What activities and interactions bring them energy and joy? This is a great conversation to have, and it easily conveys your love and interest to get to know them in a deeper way. It also gives you as the participant the opportunity for growth and expansion. Notice what comes up for you as you engage in this process. It can trigger our insecurities and fears, which, in turn, can create opportunities for vulnerable conversations. If engaged in the right way, this process is a win for everyone involved. Not only does the person you love feel seen and understood, but you get to grow as well.

Another version of this is engaging in someone else's approach and style when it comes to day-to-day dynamics. For example, my wife and I have very different approaches to cooking food from a recipe. I tend to ignore most of the recipe and do what I want while my wife likes to follow it step by step. We used to constantly clash and have fights when we tried to cook dinner together, and we would give each other grief for not doing it the way we each thought was right. Eventually, we decided to agree ahead of time which person would lead the cooking extravaganza. Whoever was the leader got to decide the approach to making dinner and the other followed. Not only was this a great exercise in working together, but it also allowed us to deepen our awareness of each other.

There are so many examples of these types of differences in our life, and we can use them as ways to connect deeper. They are also great opportunities to check in with your ego and need to control.

Participating in someone else's version of life makes them feel loved and cared for. Even if you wouldn't naturally do something their way, the act of showing up and trying out a new approach is a powerful way to connect.

A third strategy is to go along at someone else's emotional pace and to meet them where they are in their emotional awareness. In any relationship, one person is usually faster at emotionally processing than the other. This can lead to the slower person feeling emotionally overwhelmed in certain conversations. Also, in our close relationships, we are privy to witnessing a lot of the inner workings of the people we love. This vantage point can give us access to awareness that they themselves do not yet have. Unfortunately, just because we have awareness that might help them doesn't mean that they can see what we are pointing out. Awareness about ourselves only happens when we are actively engaged in a healing process.

Learning more about the pace at which someone processes their emotions, and what they might need in order to do that, is key to having productive conversations and conveying love. This can be quite challenging for someone who already knows how they feel and what they want, because the other person may need much more time and space to process it. Also, if we are not well versed in practicing patience or if we crave a deep connection with them sooner than what's possible, the result can be a lot of discomfort.

However, practicing patience can help us grow and eventually bring out even deeper conversations and a deeper connection, which are exactly what we crave. When we're considerate of the other person, we're taking care of their needs in a loving, positive way. Eventually, we may be able to reach a compromise with regard to pace.

The last strategy is becoming a better listener. How often are we too eager to tell someone all the things on our mind, but we don't have the patience to hear what's on theirs? Practicing active listening and reflecting back what we heard them say is a powerful way to connect. Saying something like "This is what I heard you say—correct me if I'm wrong" is a very powerful way of showing people how much we care. Imagine what it would feel like if someone responded to you like this.

Another version of this practice is listening with a five- or ten-minute timer and then reflecting back what you heard. This allows you to truly hold space for someone in the present moment without having to worry about what you are going to say in response. To go deeper, you can ask engaging questions about the things they are talking about.

Being a good listener is such a powerful way to make someone feel loved and to promote good energy for everyone. Many fantastic books are available that go into much greater depth on active listening if this is a topic that you want to pursue.

Healthy Conflict and Confronting the Issues

There will always be issues and challenges in any relationship. Even if your partner (or closest people) seems perfect, and you couldn't imagine any dissatisfaction whatsoever, it's guaranteed to happen eventually. Too often, we're swept up during the honeymoon phase, thinking everything will always be easy, and we buy into the cultural myth about the perfect relationship. In reality, close relationships are amazing and rewarding, but they are also a lot of hard work. Most of the issues we run into within the dynamic are healthy and normal, including dissatisfaction, disagreements, communication breakdowns, misinterpretations, hurtful exchanges, triggers, unmet needs, and intimacy challenges, as well as outright conflicts and fights. All of these challenges give us opportunities to grow and expand ourselves. Further, they can empower us to learn how to love and care for ourselves and others in better ways. The journey may be hard to go through, but if we are willing to grow, it can ultimately create deeper intimacy and connection. Knowing how to navigate these disruptions is key to having our needs met, meeting the needs of others, and creating long-lasting, satisfying relationships.

Few of us are taught how to navigate healthy conflict or speak up directly when something isn't working for us. Most of us either have unhealthy conflicts and damage our relationships, or we avoid problems all together until we eventually blow up (or it erodes the relationship). The good news is that the healthy people in our lives want to know when we're unhappy because they care about our wellbeing. They're willing to go through hard moments to help us feel better and improve the relationship. This is a great way to gauge who is healthy and who isn't.

When something doesn't feel good, we have to find the courage to speak up and be willing to participate in healthy conflict. When we do this, we give the people in our life the chance to grow closer to us, to know us better, and to be able to show us the love they feel. As crazy as it might seem, there are people in this world who will truly love and care about us in ways that matter. It's our job to promote healthy dynamics within the relationships we have.

What follows are some tools and ideas that might help you confront relationship issues and conflicts.

Speak Up and Express Yourself Directly

One of the greatest gifts you can give someone you care about is expressing yourself directly to them. This includes expressing all of your love and affection, but also your struggles. The reason this is such a gift is that it removes any confusion or misinterpretation about your feelings. It allows for efficient discussions and resolutions. But how often do we attempt to hide our insecurities, anxieties, dissatisfactions, and disagreements? This is often because we are afraid of how our true feelings will change the way someone feels about us. However, if we don't express our authentic feelings, they will come out in other ways, including passive aggressiveness, resentment, or a lack of desire to be close to someone.

It makes perfect sense that we would be afraid to show our struggles and dissatisfactions in our relationships. Our culture promotes unhealthy and superficial ideas about what makes someone desirable, and usually this doesn't include showing our imperfections and authentic feelings. Further, in unhealthy relationships, our feelings and struggles will garner negative feedback that may very well change how the other person feels about us. What a scary and hurtful experience! Usually, we already know if this is the reaction we are going to receive. However, in healthy dynamics, being vulnerable with our feelings will most likely build deeper intimacy.

Speaking up directly is a practice in authenticity, and it requires courage. When our direct expressions are met with kind reactions, our body has the evidence it needs to embrace authenticity more often. In any healthy relationship, expressions of our struggles or what isn't working for us always contributes something positive to the dynamic because it moves us a little closer to each other. We can also go a step further and tell someone what we specifically need to feel better. This allows for an easy fix and removes any games we think we must play in order to get our needs met.

Many of the issues in our relationships are due to long-term patterns that we bring into the dynamic. We might also choose people with the emotional patterns we need to confront in order to grow and heal. Healing these patterns is a journey that requires a lot of repetition. This means being committed to revisiting the same issues many times. We must give ourselves permission to be repetitive and revisit issues until they are resolved. Further, there are usually a few big issues that cannot be resolved without the help of a therapist or coach. This is all very normal, and it shouldn't be judged as a bad sign in a relationship. This is the level of commitment that is required to create truly satisfying dynamics.

Finally, there comes a time in some of our relationships when the dynamic has served its purpose. It isn't always easy to notice this or to be honest with ourselves when it happens, but a commitment to honesty and directness means we sometimes have to end a relationship. If we don't do this, our life becomes stagnant and we are left dissatisfied. Leaving a relationship may be painful, and we may need to grieve, but it's a deeply loving act. It allows for each person to move on and find new energy that will serve them better.

An important side note: when I talk about honesty and directness, I don't mean brutal honesty. We can be kind and caring at the same time that we're honest. This reminds me of a saying I've always resonated with: "Honesty without compassion is violence."

Noticing the Red

Most of us have experienced a moment with someone when we get triggered into anger and we are no longer in reality. You stop feeling grounded or open, and you can no longer think clearly. Instead, our voice gets louder, our tone gets harsher, and we stop caring about how the other person feels. This is called being "in the red." When we cross this threshold, our ability to have a productive conversation goes out the window. We lose our ability to listen well and be reflective, and we lose touch with our desire to connect and care for the other person. Sometimes, it goes as far as thinking that the person we love is our enemy. This is how crazy being in the red can make us feel. It puts us completely out of touch with reality.

Many of us haven't practiced noticing when we're in the red, nor do we have the awareness to handle it when we do notice it. Instead of stopping conversations, we try to push through conflict and end up exhausting our energy, escalating the situation, and possibly damaging our relationship.

It's interesting how the people who are closest to us have an incredible ability to push our buttons in just the right ways. This is because we crave to be seen and understood by them, and we want them to be on the same page that we are on. We have high expectations of them and of the relationship we are in. Further, love and intimacy have this amazing ability to flush out all of our old wounds and insecurities in order for us to be able to heal them. It's no wonder that our closest relationships become the most triggering.

Creating a deep relationship with someone is also challenging because both partners bring into the dynamic different beliefs and ideas on how to approach life, different ways to get their needs met, and different past experiences that have shaped them. Further, if we're in a partnership, we deal with additional stressors like money, religion, kids, jobs, etc.

If we hadn't been brought up in such an individualistic society, one that doesn't teach us how to be a part of a healthy community, we might have an easier time overlapping our life with that of another person. But since this is not the situation, it takes considerable effort to work through the differences we bring in and to see each other's value. Remembering that our closest people are here to challenge us and help us grow into better versions of ourselves is key to having successful conflict. We need to practice noticing the love they bring into our lives and thinking of the overall health and wellness of the relationship in order to make better choices when we find ourselves in the red.

Conflict arises in healthy relationships because somewhere a breakdown in communication has taken place. When we feel understood and seen in the ways that matter to us, we remain grounded and open to the other person. Even if we don't agree with what they are saying, it doesn't mean that we can't have productive conversations. This isn't to say that every conflict can be resolved. Sometimes there are too many emotions wrapped up in a topic, and then we need to enlist help. Staying open and grounded with each other is key to staying connected while in conflict.

When we find ourselves in the red, we no longer feel heard and seen or we are caught up in a triggered emotion. At that time, the conversation has stopped being productive. When this happens, try the following strategies.

The first thing to do is build body awareness about the symptoms you have when you cross into the red. Everyone's body signals are specific to them. When I feel angry, I become harsher and colder. My clients report feeling detached, numb, disengaged, or rageful. They might raise their voice, say things designed to hurt, shut down emotionally, have an emotional breakdown, have an anxiety attack, storm out, or want to win the fight at all costs, just to name a few. Notice when you go from caring and feeling open to feeling closed off and no longer caring about the other person. These are universal indicators that you've crossed the threshold into the red.

Once you learn your signals, try to notice them in the moment when they show up. This is no easy feat, because the momentum of a conflict can be strong and addictive. How often do we arrive at some point in a conflict where we don't care about anything besides winning or hurting the other person in some way? The only way to break out of that cycle is to remind ourselves of the love we have for the person we are fighting with. Do we really want to hurt them and our precious relationship? You can also recall past fights that didn't go well and how you felt afterwards. No one likes to wake up the next day feeling exhausted, emotionally hungover, depressed, and regretful about the things they said. It's such a waste of our time. When we decide to conserve our energy and preserve our relationship, we have options as to what to do next.

The second strategy, when we notice we've entered the red, is to stop the conversation and walk away. This doesn't mean that the conversation is over, and we don't need to walk away in a harsh manner. But we do have to be honest with ourselves that the dialogue is no longer productive and nothing helpful will happen until we calm down. This can be hard to do because there may be a longing in our body to try and solve the problem immediately or to lash out to quell our anger. It also hurts to disconnect from the other person, and it can feel scary to have them be upset with us. But calming down and resetting is the biggest gift we can give our relationship in these moments.

Sometimes, we need ten minutes; other times, we need days to reset. But we have to be honest about when we're truly ready to talk. Otherwise, we will cause the same fight to start again.

It's also important to make clear agreements and give reassurances. The agreements can be on how much time we'll take away and when we'll return to try to resolve the conflict. Reassurances can include "I love you, and we will figure this out" or "I need space, but I'll return." The reason for saying these things is that we care about our people and don't want them to think we no longer care about them, even if we're pissed off. This allows for productive space without the activation of panic and fear. We can also request reassurances and agreements from them.

When we return to the conversation, we need to come back with a clear head. Ask yourself two questions: "Do I love and care about this person?" and "Does this person love and care about me?" If the answer is "yes," then you should be invested in having the relationship continue and flourish, and this should influence how you are going to approach them. If you have doubts about whether there's love or care, that would be a great place to start the conversation. You might need to reassure each other that you both care. Or maybe in reality the relationship isn't good for either of you; if this is true, the conflicts will never end.

The third strategy is practicing your active listening skills. Set a timer for each person to speak. Listen for what the other person needs, why their opinions or feelings are important to them, and what you can do to help them feel better. Reflect back what you heard and get confirmation that you've accurately heard everything they said. Then switch.

Fourth, when having conflict, you should abide by "fair fighting rules." These are things that are not allowed during fights: screaming, cursing, bringing up irrelevant past topics, hitting, and storming out without reassurances and agreements are some examples. If you haven't set up fair fighting rules, that would be a great thing to do during a time when the relationship is in a good space. These rules are meant to keep fights productive and healthy, and when they're not abided by, they become indicators of when someone is in the red. Agreeing on fair fighting rules is a way to commit to a healthy and positive relationship, which increases the possibility of healthy conflict.

The fifth strategy is coming to some sort of compromise. This is no easy task because we all want to have everything we desire. And, typically, we don't practice letting go of certain things to please someone else. But we need to start thinking of the overall health of the relationship, not just ourselves. This is what's required in healthy, close relationships. Ultimately, healthy compromise helps us grow and become better versions of ourselves.

Here are a few questions to ask yourself when working on a compromise:

What am I willing to compromise in order to meet the needs of the other person?

What *can't* I compromise on?

What do I absolutely need to remain open and grounded?

What do I need to receive in order to feel like the compromise is good enough?

These questions can help you soften enough to resolve the issue.

Many of us aren't well versed in compromise. We're used to getting our way, so we can have unfair expectations regarding what we deserve in order to resolve the conflict. We aren't practiced enough in asking "When do I have enough?" Part of our growth is realizing that we can still be happy and feel loved when we don't get our way a hundred percent of the time. It's important to notice whether we have a perfectionist mentality and to realize that this characteristic isn't balanced. This mindset will get in the way of our relationships, which need to be satisfying for everyone involved.

Despite these strategies and tools, there are some topics in relationships that can't be solved without help. There is no shame in this—it happens in almost every close relationship. Having a third party who can hold a grounded and fair space for everyone is an extremely efficient way of resolving certain issues. We know what these topics are because when we try to solve them, no matter how calm and grounded we try to be, we always end up in a fight. Save yourself the wasted energy of trying to solve it by yourselves. Be willing to get help!

When choosing a third party, find someone who isn't activated by the topics you're trying to resolve. This should also be someone who is emotionally aware enough to see multiple sides. That way, everyone can feel heard and have their needs met enough to become happy with the outcome.

Repairing Damage

When we do damage in a relationship (which is inevitable at least to some degree), it's important to do what we can to repair it. Everyone hurts each other unintentionally—even the kindest, most loving people. But the good news is, most things can be repaired if we are willing to go through the healing process.

To repair a damaged relationship, we first must be open to self-reflection and feedback. We must be willing to hear when someone tells us that our behavior was hurtful or scary. These are not easy things to hear because we have to confront our imperfections and flaws, aspects of ourselves that might make us feel ashamed. And we have to grieve the fact that we have hurt the people we love. But this is what it takes to rebuild and heal. The feedback is a main function of having close relationships because it helps us transform into the best versions of ourselves. We just need the courage to listen to it. I know I'm guilty of rageful outbursts with my wife and kids that have caused them to feel scared of me. It always triggers deep shame in me and a desire to do better.

The second tool for repairing relationships is having empathy for the people we are close with and putting ourselves in their shoes. Each of us experiences the relationship in different ways, and we have to be willing to understand what their version is and what they need in order to feel loved.

Shifting certain behaviors can be hard on our ego, especially if we are used to doing everything the way we want. But being in healthy relationships requires less selfish thinking and more growth towards the overall health of the people involved. This is where love and connection can really flourish.

Third, nothing is more powerful for repairing a relationship than ownership and apologizing. Statements like "I'm sorry for how I made you feel. I understand why that was hurtful to you, and I'm willing to change" can be very powerful ways to repair. Or we can simply say "You were right, I was wrong, and I apologize." These are acts of love that can be enormously healing if said sincerely.

It's never too late to try to repair a relationship. Most people tend to be very forgiving if we apologize, acknowledge the problem, and own up to our mistakes. Don't believe it's too late to fix a conflict or heal hurt feelings. Time is irrelevant when it comes to spreading love, and being willing to repair our relationships is a deeply loving act.

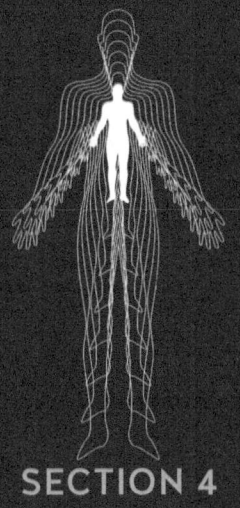

PLANT MEDICINES AND OTHER HEALINGS

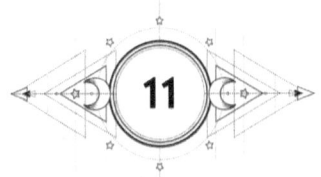

BENEFICIAL HEALING MODALITIES

E ven though my healing journey involved a lot of pain and struggle, I have to say that I've enjoyed the process. In my determination to find the awareness I needed and to heal my issues, I've been fortunate to personally experience a lot of amazing healing modalities. Each one had its time and place in my life, and some I resonated with more than others, but they all offered something powerful and interesting.

This book wouldn't feel complete without acknowledging and discussing many of these modalities so that you can consider them for yourself. The journey of healing is a lifelong commitment to growth and deepening within yourself. No one tool will ever be enough to give you everything you need. Instead, stay open to trying out whatever opportunities the universe puts in your path, as long as they feel healthy and safe for you. I hope you find these modalities interesting and intriguing.

THERAPY/COACHING. As I've mentioned throughout the book, I had about four years of therapy, and I saw a coach for another two years before that. My wife and I also did couples therapy for over a year when our marriage needed support, and we just returned to couples therapy again this year. The different practitioners were truly transformative in helping me build emotional awareness and heal my emotional wounds. I truly love therapy and coaching, and I'm committed to always having some form of it in my life. As long as you find someone who makes you feel understood and comfortable, healing can happen. One resource that I've found extremely helpful in finding a therapist is *Psychology Today*'s database on their website. You can search in any zip code with any insurance, and you can even indicate specialties. With regard to life coaches, every practitioner's style is different. In the coaching sessions that I offer, I tend to focus on emotional and spiritual healing, while some providers are more goal-oriented. Similar to finding the right therapist, find a coach whose methods resonate with you, help you build awareness and make you feel empowered.

THE RECONNECTION/MATRIX ENERGETICS. I was introduced to both of these versions of energy healing through my mother, who is one of my channels that the universe uses to guide me and send me messages. She took me to the Reconnection training Level 1 when I was 17 years old, which was incredible. The Reconnection is a type of energy medicine and quantum healing that reconnects people to their soul's essence of love and light. Once we're connected back to the source, spontaneous and profound healings can happen. You can read more about this in Eric Pearl's book, *The Reconnection*.

Matrix Energetics is another example of quantum healing with a different approach. I attended the Level 1 and 2 trainings and found it to be a wonderful method. Energy is shifted with the use of many energetic tools and belief systems, and profound healings have been recorded. You can read more about this work in Richard Bartlett's book, *Matrix Energetics: The Science and Art of Transformation*.

There are many energy medicines out there, including

acupuncture, which I do in my practice, as well as modalities like Reiki. These can be very powerful tools that we should all be open to exploring. One caution that I will add is that sometimes people get caught in a trap and believe that these energy modalities will heal all of their problems. This is never the case because no one tool will solve everything for us. We should be cautious around anyone who claims to be able to heal all of our problems.

ACUPUNCTURE/CHINESE MEDICINE. As a Chinese medicine practitioner, I may be biased when it comes to my opinion about acupuncture and Chinese medicine, but this is an incredible healing modality with a vast range of helpful tools. Chinese medicine is an ancient form of physical, emotional, and energetic healing that has been practiced for thousands of years. It is a huge category of medicine equivalent to the vastness of western medicine.

Acupuncture is a healing modality within Chinese medicine. Practitioners insert tiny needles into specific areas along energy channels called meridians. Each meridian is associated with an organ system, like the liver meridian, and therefore it has a very specific function in the body. The sensation of needle insertion is not a sharp stabbing feeling like when blood is drawn at the doctor's office. Instead, either the needles are not felt at all or a mellow achiness may be associated with them. Acupuncture points are chosen specifically to move stagnant energy, to remove pain, to soothe the nervous system, or to tonify the body, just to name a few. Once the needles are placed in the body, the client rests on the table for at least 15 to 20 minutes and oftentimes falls asleep.

Acupuncture is incredibly effective for so many physical and emotional ailments. I will mention the most common conditions that I treat in my practice. The first is removing body pain.

Acupuncture is great at treating any body pain you can think of. This includes headaches, migraines, neck and back pain, premenstrual cramps, knee pain, hip pain, and sciatica, to name just a few. Acupuncture also has a wonderful soothing effect on the nervous system, and it is very effective for treating aliments like anxiety, depression, insomnia, trauma responses, and acute/chronic stress. Other common things clients use acupuncture for are infertility, digestive complaints, allergies, nerve pain, numbness, asthma, and bell's palsy.

Acupuncture combined with other modalities like cupping and Chinese herbal medicine greatly enhances the effectiveness and long-lasting impact of the treatments. Further, in my practice, I combine acupuncture with coaching to offer clients simultaneous emotional and physical healing. I have watched transformative things happen with this combination.

Chinese herbal medicine is another huge category that is not as commonly used in America as it is in other countries, partially because many Americans don't tolerate the strong tastes of the teas. However, Chinese herbs are incredible at healing the body in so many ways, and I encourage everyone to give them a try.

As with any modality, in Chinese medicine, every practitioner has their own style and approach, so find someone that you resonate with. Additionally, many insurance carriers now cover acupuncture in the United States as part of the yearly benefits.

SHAMANIC CEREMONIES. The four shamanic ceremonies I describe below are found in many indigenous and native cultures around the world. Each shaman performs these ceremonies differently. I describe below only the versions that I have experienced. Also, around the world, there are many names for a person who performs spiritual/energetic healings and who holds a spiritual space for the community. Shaman is the most common term used in Western culture and I use it here as a general term. However, I encourage people to be respectful of the ceremonies in any culture and to use the proper terminology within the community.

SOUL RETRIEVALS. During this healing, a shaman goes into the spiritual realms and retrieves parts of your spirit that were lost due to trauma or for other reasons. They also remove things from your body that aren't yours and that belong to other people like energies that have become attached to you. They can help to get rid of old thinking patterns, heal emotional wounds, heal past life patterning and trauma, and resolve other issues.

Soul retrieval is a big ceremony, sometimes lasting four to six hours, and it takes a person at least a year to integrate and process all that happens within a session. Usually, there is an intake period before the ceremony, where the shaman learns about your intentions, who you are, and your life history. After the ceremony, there's a debriefing in which the shaman tells you all the relevant information they discovered on the journey. This includes the soul parts that were brought back to you. You then work with the shaman to build a plan for integrating these soul parts over the next year. For example, in my latest soul retrieval, my infant self and my five-year-old self were brought back to me.

I've had three soul retrievals in the past ten years, and each one has been deeply transformative. In my most recent ceremony, which was last year, I was helped with removing a lot of grief and trauma that was still in my body from past family dynamics, and my relationship with the Divine Mother was strengthened and deepened. Also, as I said above, my infant and five-year-old self were returned to me. These parts returning have been key to the exponential spiritual deepening I've been experiencing since the ceremony. A lot of my old memories and feelings have come back, which has helped me return to passions I had forgotten about. These include my deep passion for energetic and spiritual medicines. I have also felt more inner peace in my mind and body, which has allowed me to reduce stress overall and be a better partner, father, and healer.

When you look for a shamanic practitioner who offers these services, be sure to find someone who has been trained by a teacher associated with an indigenous lineage. Practitioners need to be taught how to conduct these ceremonies, and it must be with the permission of a teacher who has a respectful relationship with their ancestors and this medicine.

SWEAT LODGE CEREMONY. This is a very powerful and challenging ceremony where you respectfully enter a hut or tent that's completely covered with a material that withstands extreme heat and blocks out all light. Everyone sits around the center pit of the hut, where red hot stones are rolled in during each round of the ceremony. These stones have been heated in a fire for many hours beforehand and are raging hot. Once the stones are rolled into the pit, the door is closed, leaving everyone in complete darkness. Each round of the sweat lodge has a different healing intention associated with it, such as healings for yourself, for loved ones, and for the Earth.

The sweat lodge is meant to replicate the experience of going into the Earth's core, which reconnects us with our deep relationship with Mother Earth and with our ancestral spirits. It's also where we're cleansed and healed, we have deep spiritual experiences, and we find new depths of personal strength.

We find this strength by actively praying to our spiritual helpers and ancestors in the sweat lodge. Even if you don't know who your spirits are, you can pray to the good, true, and beautiful helping spirits or ancestral spirits who are with you.

Active prayer protects you from the heat and helps you build the strength you need to get through each round.

Once the doors are closed, people say their intentions or prayers out loud. Then, water is poured on the stones, releasing a lot of hot steam. Traditional songs are sung to bring in helping and healing spirits, to create the proper energy, and to remind everyone that we're connected to each other, the spiritual realm, and the Earth. These songs can also be very helpful for withstanding the heat.

Once the prayers and songs have been sung and the shaman feels that the round is complete, the door is opened so that fresh air can come in. This also provides a chance for people to leave the lodge if they're struggling to handle the heat. They can choose to come back into the hut when the next round begins or remain outside.

When the next round starts, more hot stones are rolled into the center pit, the door is closed, and the process begins again. Every shaman conducts a sweat lodge in a different way and chooses how many rounds to include, as well as how long each round will last.

I recommend keeping your eyes open while in the darkness, because you might "see" powerful things through this healing process.

Never do a sweat lodge with anyone who isn't trained by a reputable teacher, because these practices can be very dangerous. People have died in sweat lodges. A proper leader of these ceremonies knows how to take care of the group and make sure everyone is safe.

DEPOSSESSION. Due to Christian teachings and images from movies, there's a lot of baggage surrounding the idea of possessions. The imagery associated with people being possessed tends to be terrifying. This is not typical of what a possession looks like and how a depossession ceremony works. In reality, spirits can enter our body for a variety of reasons. Usually, it's because we aren't taking up the full space of our body, which can happen at times during trauma, addiction, or drug use. Most of us haven't been taught how to spiritually and energetically protect ourselves, which can sometimes cause this to happen too. But unlike the horror films we watch, most people aren't aware it's happening to them.

Ceremonies like soul retrievals or depossessions can remove these entities from us. I experienced a depossession, and the spirit was very willing to leave my body and go back to the spirit world. It didn't seem to want to cause me problems (which is not to say that people can't have more intense versions of this experience). Properly trained shamans can perform ceremonies like this and check in with their guides to see if a possession is happening.

HOUSE BLESSINGS. I love house blessings because they're a beautiful way to clear a space of old or negative energies, replacing them with good intentions and love. This ceremony is similar to a soul retrieval, but it's done for the spirit of the land and spirit of our home, our workplace, or other spaces.

An altar is set up in the main part of the space, and the people who occupy the home stay by the altar, singing, dancing, and sending intentions through it. The altar is essentially a portal that sends this energy to the shaman so that they can use it to fill the space back up with good vibes after they've cleared negative or unwanted energy. Working with a drummer and their spirit guides, the shaman moves through the space and is shown energies, entities, and other things that aren't wanted in each room of the home. With the help of their spiritual team and other spiritual tools, they remove these energies and replace them with the energy coming through the altar from those in attendance.

Intentions are set ahead of time, along with an intake about the history of the house and land and what has happened there. After the ceremony, there's a debriefing with a big, festive meal for everyone. Protections are also placed around the house and the land in order to maintain the positive energy and keep the negative away.

I've had house blessings in most of the places I've lived and noticed a big difference afterwards.

Two great books that dive deeper into these topics are *The Way of the Shaman* and *The Cave and the Cosmos* by Michael Harner. Also, many of Sandra Ingerman's books including *Soul Retrieval* and *The Book of Ceremony*. Further, you can check out my mentor's website if you are interested in studying this form of medicine: Char Sundust and The Sundust Oracle Institute.

HYPNOSIS. Most people are familiar with hypnosis since it's more generally accepted in western culture as a form of healing. It's a method for ending old patterns of thinking, stopping addictions, retraining the unconscious, finding old memories so that we can heal wounds, and past life regressions, to name a few. A lot of people have found hypnosis to be a powerful modality for their healing. I've done many sessions in my life, but I didn't find it to be a particularly healing modality for me. However, I do know many clients who have loved it.

One of my all-time favorite books, which involves past life regression, is a great resource for learning more about hypnosis: *Many Lives, Many Masters* by Dr. Brian Weiss.

BIRTH CHART READINGS/ASTROLOGY. These days, it seems like everyone knows their astrological sign and how it explains their behavior and personality. I'm not a big fan of the popularized version of astrology, but if you can get your entire chart read by a true expert, it can be a transformative experience. There's so much we can learn about our life path and struggles when we do a birth chart reading and learn about our astrological signs.

Experienced astrologers can do other kinds of readings as well, including ones for the upcoming year, for business adventures, and for relationships.

TAROT. I do quite a bit of tarot reading in my coaching sessions, and it always seems to evoke powerful conversations and insights. There are endless varieties of tarot cards out there and a lot of different belief systems about how to interpret them. If you buy your own deck, find one that really calls to you, including images you resonate with. And when working with a tarot reader make sure you find someone you trust. The basic idea behind tarot is that the cards give you clarity about different aspects of yourself and your life. You can ask endless questions, and the cards will reflect the most pertinent information you need in the moment. I find it helpful to have someone else interpret the cards for me, because a lot of the time, I get in my own way.

Oracle cards and other types of decks, which are similar to tarot cards, also provide information. You can buy them online and use your body to determine which decks you're drawn to.

MEDIUMSHIP. This is an interesting modality that I love, but unfortunately, it comes with a lot of baggage. There's a long history of people claiming to talk to spirits who are actually just greedy people with big egos. But there are true mediums out there who serve as a bridge between the worlds to bring us healing and wisdom. Even within the shamanic community that I'm a part of, talking to spirits is very common.

Going to see an authentic medium can be a profound experience. There's something about connecting to our loved ones who have passed or connecting to the spirit world that meets a deep need within us. One of my favorite mediums of all time is George Anderson. His books are incredible.

When trying out a medium, use your body and intuition to tell you if they're a good person for you to work with. Remember that just because someone says what we want to hear, it doesn't mean they're the real deal. We want to work with people who empower us and keep us grounded.

SOMA/STRUCTURAL INTEGRATION/FASCIAL RELEASE MASSAGE/ROLFING. I trained in somatic massage in order to offer more effective treatments to my clients, and I've always been drawn to fascial release work as a part of healing. Soma Structural Integration® (SSI) is a process of resetting the fascial system to heal body pain, enhance mobility, provide better balance, and improve overall wellness. Usually, this is done in a series of 11 treatments, with each appointment focusing on resetting a certain part of the fascial system.

I was trained in Somassage, which is a 90-minute, full-body, fascial-release massage. SSI is a direct descendant of Ida Rolf and the rolfing massage modality. SOMA is magical for many reasons, and I've watched transformations happen on my table. When I did the 11-part series for my own healing, I noticed a deep change in my physical body.

TAI CHI/QI GONG. These are powerful, ancient modalities that are becoming more popular in the United States, but they've existed for a long time in countries like China, Japan, and Korea. These energetic traditions have a long history and knowledge base similar to that of martial arts and yoga. Both of these modalities involve building up different types of energy in the body and directing the movement of energy internally for physical and emotional healing, stress reduction, and regulation of the nervous system.

These practices are usually taught in a class led by an instructor. As you practice and become more familiar with the movements, you will deepen your awareness and influence on the energy in your body. Both of these modalities have endless aspects to be mastered, so people who are drawn to them may spend a lifetime learning them.

We were required to take a lot of Tai Chi and Qi Gong classes in acupuncture school, so I experienced the effects of both. I loved how I felt after practicing them and can see how they could be very powerful tools for sustainable health and healing.

WIM HOF. Wim's cold plunge and breathing methods have gathered a massive worldwide following, and for good reason. They're very effective! His offerings, based on ancient knowledge, are unique and interesting. After charging up the body with breathing techniques, he shows people how to breathe appropriately while sitting in frigid water. The intensity of the cold not only strengthens the body, but also facilitates physical, emotional, and mental healing. I took his Level 1 training and have been doing both the breathing practices and the cold plunges and cold showers for more than a year now. I love it! You can read more in his book, *The Wim Hof Method.*

AYAHUASCA. Many indigenous cultures around the world have used ayahuasca (or another psychoactive plant) for a long time, but each group has a different relationship with it. The shaman who performed my ceremonies was trained in the Shipibo tribe, and the descriptions in the introduction of this book and below are based on my personal experiences. As I wrote in my introduction, I can't say enough positive things about ayahuasca. Going through these ceremonies deeply transformed my life and healed wounds that I never thought could be healed. It also helped me reconnect to universal love, my love for my family, and my love for the Earth. I was fortunate to work with a shaman who was trained in the Amazon to use the medicine properly. I think this is crucial when using any plant medicine with this power. If you want to learn more, I recommend reading *The Fellowship of the River* by Joseph Tafur. He wrote about this medicine while studying with the Shipibo tribe.

PSILOCYBIN/LSD. These are mind-altering medicines that many people have found to be enormously healing if taken properly. Too often, however, they're used as party drugs, so their healing potential is wasted. With the right intentions and environment, they can be powerful tools for healing. My general sense of both of these medicines is that they help people reconnect to love and something bigger than themselves, which is really the medicine we all need to heal. I haven't tried LSD, but some of my clients have, and they reported that it was helped them a lot. I have used mushrooms and was impressed by the level of insight and healing they gave me. Michael Pollan has great books on this subject, including *This is Your Mind on Plants* and *How to Change Your Mind*.

MARIJUANA. I'm thankful that marijuana has been widely accepted in the United States and mostly decriminalized. It's a powerful and wonderful plant medicine. Just like any other, however, its effectiveness depends on the quality of the plant, how it's used, how much is used, and the person's intentions while using it. My experience has been that it can help regulate anxiety, get rid of pain, help with appetite, regulate seizures, and soothe stress, among other things.

However, I do think it's overused in the same way that we overuse modern western medications. Therefore, it can cause unwanted effects. A lot of people use marijuana every day for years on end, a practice that I fundamentally disagree with. It's too powerful to be ingested or smoked for a lifetime. Instead, we're meant to use it alongside other healing modalities and lifestyle challenges to create positive shifts. Marijuana deserves our respect, and it should be used with the right intentions.

TOBACCO. This is an incredibly sacred and powerful plant that countless indigenous cultures use in unique ways. However, people have a long and clear history of misusing it in many disrespectful and irresponsible ways, which is why it causes so many diseases. Tobacco has many uses as a medicine and sacred herb, and I can only speak to my experiences using it during healing ceremonies.

Tobacco can be used as a sacred offering to spirit and the Earth to show respect and gratitude, but also to ask for healing, help, and protection. In some traditions, when smoked, it can carry our thoughts and intentions to the creator and help us manifest what's in our mind. It can also be used to clear energy, whether the smoke is blown on someone or whether someone bathes with it.

When I was taking part in the ayahuasca ceremonies, tobacco was used as snuff when someone needed help to clear stuck energy in their body. I also shared a ceremonial pipe with my shamanic community after a ceremony. The way to build a good relationship with tobacco is to approach it with respect and to listen carefully as to how it should be used. This powerful plant can be a wonderful ally if used appropriately.

DIET. I can't express enough the importance of eating a healthy, well-rounded diet. Quality food is the foundation for our physical, emotional, and mental health. I was fortunate to be brought up by a mother who is an amazing nutritionist. She knows a great deal about the complexities of food. Without her knowledge, I would have been very sick due to my dairy intolerance, among other things.

Unfortunately, we have made food tremendously complicated. There are endless topics like non-GMOs, organic food, gluten intolerance, and food allergies, as well as all sorts of diets such as low-carb, vegan, Paleo, Keto, and on and on. This causes a lot of confusion and creates doubt in our ability to have an intuitive relationship with the food we eat

In my practice, I promote a simple approach that involves a well-rounded diet full of organic fruits and vegetables, plus proteins and grains of various kinds. Not everyone has the resources to buy organic food, so I work with people on what foods they have access too. I'm also a big believer in elimination diets for anyone who thinks they might have a food allergy or food sensitivity. Many great books increase awareness about food, including *Salt, Sugar, Fat* by Michael Moss, *In Defense of Food* by Michal Pollan, *Wheat Belly* by William David, *What Your Food Ate* by David Montgomery and Anne Bikle, and my mother's book, *Cure Your Child with Food* by Kelly Dorfman. These books are just on the tip of the iceberg when it comes to knowledge around eating.

CONCLUSION

I f anyone had told me 10 years ago that I would one day feel complete gratitude for this healing journey, I would have laughed in their face. I was so alone in my suffering, and I felt too complicated and intense for anyone to understand. I was also so angry about my suffering because I felt that I had done nothing wrong to deserve it. I never would have imagined a reality where my suffering was gone and I felt thankful.

But the universe has this beautiful ability to change our lives. Looking back, I see how each part of my process was perfectly orchestrated for me to gain the depth and awareness I truly needed in order to help others. Without my suffering and my determination to find healing solutions, I would not have earned the emotional tools I can now offer to all of my clients and anyone who reads this book. These tools, along with the deep connections I experience with clients, are incredibly valuable to me.

This process has also given me access to live a life of deep meaning and purpose, something that endlessly feeds my soul. This in turn has provided me access to a rich spiritual life, which I also truly treasure. All of this, plus the love of my wife and children, make it easy to feel gratitude for the journey.

My hope is that this book awakens something deep and true in everyone who reads it. Our bodies are extremely intelligent, spiritually attuned, and trustworthy. Learning to trust all the ways our body communicates to us is a deeply transformative and healing process. We all need help learning how to do this, but once this shift happens, there is no turning back. Nothing brings more inner peace than ending the fight with yourself.

This healing journey is a process that awakens us to love in all its glorious forms. Creating healthy love is what life is all about. Love is a powerful force that is designed to challenge us to evolve in deep ways. It also leads us to a life full of meaning.

I wish you love and support on your healing journey.

ACKNOWLEDGEMENTS

There are so many people in my life who have truly helped me heal and grow and become the healthy man I am today.

I first want to say thank you to my amazing wife, Sashya, who has provided me with enormous unconditional love that has allowed me to feel safe and find myself again. I am so grateful to have found you, somebody I fully trust and can be my authentic self with. You have pushed me to grow in a million different ways, which has made me a better person, and I am grateful that you love me despite all my bullshit. I know our journey has been a lot of work, but I love you and truly appreciate all that you are. You are a wonderful partner and amazing mother. Thank you for your dedication to our relationship and our family.

I am so grateful for my children, Melody and Skye, who have such lust for life, creativity, and playfulness. Thank you for pushing me to step into my role as a father, which has helped me to be more playful and to grow in deep ways that I never thought possible.

I am very grateful for both of my parents, Kelly and Jeff, who invested a lot of time, money, and energy into helping me find myself, heal, and flourish. Both of you worked tirelessly to set me up for a successful life, both financially and emotionally. I am truly grateful for this. I want to send my appreciation to my mom for being a great role model when it comes to being an authentic healer. Watching you practice in my early life, and having conversations about your work and the work I wanted to do, have given me a huge advantage to become the healer I am today.

I want to send my love and gratitude to my dog, Rockstar. You came into my life at a time when I desperately needed love and a companion, and you rescued me from the loneliness and despair I was experiencing. Thank you for being such a healing and loving companion. And thank you for teaching me so much about leadership and what it means to be a healthy leader. Our struggles together, and the healing we went through, seemed to awaken this leadership awareness within me, something I still use to this day. I love you and miss you and send you my blessings.

Another key person in my life was Warren, the original creator of our book group, "Practicing Living in the Moment." I am so grateful for his desire to create a group where we could grow and be vulnerable together. Thank you, Warren, for creating this space. It truly rescued me from a dark place and put me back on the path I needed to be on. Thank you for your vulnerable conversations and for helping me open up to new spiritual and emotional depths. And thank you for seeing my leadership potential and for gently pushing me into this role. I grew a lot from being in that amazing community, and I am truly grateful for the catalyst you were in my life. Finally, thank you for coming into my dreams when I was in rough shape and for holding me and helping me find hope. Your visits were magical, and they always came at just the right time. I hope you are flourishing and doing well, and I send you my deepest love and gratitude.

I am very grateful for three healers who helped to transform my inner world and trauma. My shadow coach, Martha, and my therapists, John and Jamie. All of you contributed so much in terms of healing my relationship with myself and helping me to build the awareness I needed around family dynamics, attachment theory, and how intelligent my body is. Thank you for the incredible work you do and the commitment you have to connecting with your clients in deep and loving ways.

I want to give gratitude to the two shamans (who shall remain nameless) who hold sacred plant medicine ceremonies on their property. My times with both of you were truly transformative and opened up a whole new world for me in terms of spiritual healing. Thank you for your dedication to these ceremonies, because I know it takes a lot of hard work to always provide this space. I feel so honored to have been able to participate in multiple ceremonies when most people have never even heard of this medicine. Further, I know it takes a lot of courage to provide this medicine, and that it is a risk you are willing to take in order to bring healing to so many people who need it. Thank you for following your calling in order to do this.

Another person who I want to acknowledge is my mentor, Sharlean Windus. Thank you, Sharlean, for being an awesome mentor, for holding a very powerful space for me to deepen my energetic and spiritual awareness, and for helping me step fully into my authentic self. I love your approach to this medicine and your creativity, and I appreciate how you only do the things that feel right and throw away the rest. I also appreciate your intense dedication to endlessly going deep and your commitment to self-growth. Your intensity matches mine in a way that makes me feel at ease. It's a medicine for my soul. I always leave your office clearheaded and fully in my power, which is an amazing feeling.

Char Sundust is another person for whom I am deeply grateful. Thank you, Char, for teaching me and so many other people the wisdom of your lineages. Your dedication to spirit and waking up the sacred in all of us is truly incredible. Being a part of your classes and the bigger community was and continues to be the catalyst I truly needed to own my authentic self and to commit deeply to my purpose. You were transformative in making this book happen and in helping me find my writing style so that my ideas could flow through me with ease. I feel truly honored to be working with you and your family of healers, and to be able to participate in such incredible and life-changing ceremonies. Thank you for all you provide to this world.

Last, I need to acknowledge all of my spiritual allies including all of my healthy ancestor spirits, my power animals and animal allies, my angel spirits, my guardians and protectors, grandmother sun, father sky, beautiful moon spirit, and the good, true, and beautiful spirits of the four winds, the four ways, the four directions, and the four elements. Also, Divine Earth Mother and Divine Mother. I feel so blessed by each and every one of you and the relationship I am graced to have with all of you. You have all helped me so much through this intense journey I am committed to, one that has been so powerful and transformative, and that forced me to find my strength and build the awareness I needed in order to be of service to this world. Thank you for always helping me stay attuned to the light and my purpose on Earth. Thank you for being with me, guiding me, helping me, and helping all of our clients. I trust you completely and I am so grateful to be a team with you.